Allison's writing is high on colour and is packed with engaging accounts of the sort of things that are just another day at the office for the average safari guide. If you love the thrill of safaris this book is for you. It is full of hair-raising stories of escape and adventure in the bush. Having worked for more than twenty years in Botswana, South Africa, Namibia and Mozambique, the stars of Allison's show are hungry lions and territorial hippos. There are some white-knuckle tales of dodging landmines too...

Sunday Telegraph

This is a wry and immensely colourful account of a young man's adventures as a safari leader in Botswana. Scared of heights, unfamiliar with the gym and terrified of an innocuous little tree-frog, high school drop-out Peter's rapport with the job is not immediately obvious... A hugely eloquent writer in spite of severe mid-safari injuries to the head, he masterfully paces suspense. You'll never look at an innocent safari tour the same way again. Hapless and shamelessly self-deprecating, he possesses the asset of a perfect story teller – the ability to poke fun at himself. Witty, exciting and ultimately unmissable.

Real Travel

ALSO BY PETER ALLISON

Don't Run, Whatever You Do: My Adventures as a Safari Guide

How to Walk a Puma: & other things I learned while stumbing around South America

Don't Look
BEHIND YOU!

True Tales of a Safari Guide

PETER ALLISON

NICHOLAS BREALEY
PUBLISHING

London • Boston

This edition first published in Great Britain by
Nicholas Brealey Publishing in 2019
An imprint of John Murray Press

An Hachette company

First published in Great Britain by Nicholas Brealey Publishing in 2009

1

British Library Cataloguing-in-Publication Data
A catalogue record for this book is available from the British Library.

ISBN 978 1 52930 937 9
eBook ISBN 978 1 85788 417 3

Text designer: Sheryl P. Kober
Layout artist: Kim Burdick

Printed and bound in Great Britain by Clays Ltd, Elcograf S.p.A.

John Murray Press policy is to use papers that are natural, renewable
and recyclable products and made from wood grown in sustainable forests.
The logging and manufacturing processes are expected to conform to
the environmental regulations of the country of origin.

Nicholas Brealey Publishing   Nicholas Brealey Publishing
John Murray Press   Hachette Book Group
Carmelite House   Market Place Center
50 Victoria Embankment   53 State Street
London, EC4Y 0DZ, UK   Boston, MA 02109, USA
Tel: 020 3122 6000   Tel: (617) 263 1834

www.nicholasbrealey.com

This book is again dedicated to anyone who works to preserve wild places—from those who live in uncomfortable conditions in the field to teach us more about animals, to people who take a little time to lobby for protection of wilderness, my good friends in the safari business, and even the legislators who sign national parks into existence. They all make some sacrifice for this, and I salute them.

CONTENTS

ACKNOWLEDGMENTS

This list must always start with Flavia, whose patience and love give me a foundation that I can work from. Not many people would tolerate hearing these stories a hundred times and then endure reading them, but she does just that with good humor and many servings of pasta.

My hardworking agent Kate Epstein takes care of so many things that I am no good at, but beyond that is also a great friend and mentor.

Holly Rubino at The Globe Pequot Press was sent a rather drab first draft and patiently guided me toward what you hold here, for which I am very grateful and hope you will be too.

This book was not written in any one place—some in my home in Sydney, but much while I was on the road. Many people had me in their homes at this point, and I must thank Attie and Christina Jonker—hosts so generous and kind I suggest you track them down and befriend them, then stay at their place; you won't want to leave. Iva Spitzer saved me from the bankruptcy that staying in New York would have brought about, and did it in great style while we swapped many an African story. Devlin Foxcroft showed that despite his many bad habits (really, who drinks beer from a shoe?) he is a great friend to have and put me up in Johannesburg. Thanks also to Alta from his office at Impulse Getaways for arranging so much.

The people in the 5 x 5 social room (you know who you are) gave me a welcome distraction when I was blocked, but just as often when I should have been working. Any mistakes I missed during the edits can be squarely blamed on them.

Lastly, I've had family support not just from my wonderful sister Laurie, but also from Susie and the late Renzo Abbate. We all miss you, Renzo.

INTRODUCTION

Writing is a dangerous game.

In 2007 I wrote a book called *Don't Run, Whatever You Do*. Seeing it published gave me a triple thrill. It made me a fourth-generation writer on my mother's side, it fulfilled a lifelong ambition to become an author, and lastly but not of least significance, it put some money in my pocket. The check sent to me was for an amount meager to most, but able to cover my rent for some time.

When I went to deposit the check at a suburban bank branch in Sydney, the teller smiled back at me in the professional way that bank tellers do. But as she studied the check, the façade began to crack a little, and then crumble. I just stood there, grinning broadly, unaware that she was reaching for the silent alarm.

My fiancée, standing beside me, was far sharper, and leaned forward. "It's the title of a book," she said softly. "This is his first payment as a writer."

I took a while to register what Flavia had said, and to interpret the look of horror that was now fading to vague suspicion on the face of the cashier.

"Oh!" I said, then "Oh!" again, just to demonstrate how articulate writers are, realizing that the book title was printed on the check. "*Don't Run!* That's not a good thing to hand over in a bank, is it?"

I wasn't arrested that day, but it was close. If I'd been by myself, I just may well have been.

So being a writer has its hazards, ones that most days I don't seem prepared for. Being a safari guide was not dissimilar. I started each day knowing that I might find a scorpion in my boot, get lost in the bush, or be charged by a lion. While I am not at all a brave man, I am fascinated by animals, and my curiosity about what might be around the next corner or what I'd see next kept me in the game for more than ten years. The stories in this book are campfire tales, the sort that safari guides tell at night, but there are also a few confessions that would never be shared with tourists.

This is not a sequel, but rather a companion volume to *Don't Run, Whatever You Do*. It starts at the start like a story should, at the beginning of my career, and hops through various stages of training, guiding, camp management, and teaching. My career began in the Sabi Sands Game Reserve of South Africa, a private section of the famous Kruger National Park. From South Africa I moved to the place that became my home, Botswana's Okavango Delta. For most of my time there I lived at a place called Mombo, an island in the middle of the world's largest oasis, which sits in the middle of the world's greatest stretch of sand. This is a place where desert animals from the Kalahari make their homes next to aquatic creatures like hippos, and where the unusual becomes commonplace. In the Delta it is possible to see some of the larger cats swimming for fun, herds of buffalo that shake the land, and a flood that comes in the middle of the dry season. There is no place like it on Earth.

These are the stories of a not particularly brave safari guide.

THREE LITTLE PIGS

I was at the bottom, looking up. Above me were safari guides, offering encouragement, telling me it was easy to get where they were. But I am a lifelong fearer of heights, to the point that I don't even enjoy standing up, and think it far more sensible to stay seated. The guides shouted out to me that I was missing out on a great view, and that they could see all sorts of wildlife and scenery from their perch on our brand-new communications tower. I wanted to join them, wanted to defeat my phobia, but after repeated failure, I could only tuck my tail between my legs and slink away.

Once the others were gone I returned to the tower and made another solo attempt. I was very proud to be three rungs higher than I had gone previously, above my own head height. My hand reached for the next rung, but instead of feeling metal I gripped something slimy. It squirmed. My hand released its hold, and for no good reason the other one did too and I fell, with just enough time to think "tree frog" before my feet hit the ground, skidded out, and my backside gave a flat *thwack* into the hard packed earth. The frog was nowhere to be seen, presumably still safe on its perch wondering why the purple-faced and sweaty creature that had grabbed it was so quick to let it go.

I looked back up the tower, wondering if I should try again, mustering courage. But just the sight of its distant tip made the sky turn, and I gave up. On this casually violent continent I was more afraid of this tower than I was of any man or animal.

"Bugger it," I said to myself, shot a last resentful glance skywards, and limped away.

◎

Three days later I was there to greet the safari vehicles as they came in from their morning drive. This was a task that was starting to gall me. I'd been training to be a guide for months, and was achingly close to my goal. Serving drinks in my role as camp bartender, never an imposition before, felt beneath me now. I yearned to be given the credibility of the neat khaki shirt and embossed epaulettes of the guides, bolstered by the machismo of driving with a rifle in front of me and the real ability to muscle the chunky four-wheel-drives around the bush. Instead I listened to Devlin as he hopped from his vehicle and announced that there were lions just outside the camp, and that I might want to warn the rest of the staff not to go past the outskirts of the structures that made up our enclave of civilization.

"Sure," I replied, immediately thinking that I'd like a look at them myself. So as soon as the pleasantries of brunch were disposed of, I sidled up to Devlin and asked exactly where he had seen the lions, and stated that I might go and get up close to them. "Not in my vehicle," he replied flatly. Devlin had been with me on many of my driving lessons, episodes of gross environmental destruction, that while unintentional still cause me guilt.

"I was thinking of walking up to them," I answered back.

"Sure you're ready for that?"

"Sure."

He shrugged, and told me the lions were beside the track that led from the back of camp, past the manager's house-shaped tent and out into the bush. It was a road tourists didn't usually see, ungraded and bumpy, low brush thick on either side of it. I passed the telephone tower as I sidled along, my breath getting choppy and irregular as nervous anticipation took hold.

These were lions that I was about to walk up to. *Lions*. It had been with the most affected indifference that I had asked Devlin where they were, as if I wasn't a suburban kid who knew just how lucky he was to have ended up here. But I was secretly buzzing with excitement, my blood gushing and pulsing to a conga beat, the small hairs on my neck stiff and bristly.

A light breeze puffed some dust from the road, and flipped leaves back and forth, flashing their pale undersides. The dust, the leaves, all seemed the color of lion, and I couldn't spot the cats that Devlin had said were in the middle of the road when he left them. If I had been more experienced I would have known that as the day heated up, the lions would move to shade. If I had been more experienced I would have listened for birds and small animals making chirrups and alarms that would have told me where the lions were. If I had been more experienced I wouldn't have walked any further, to a place where the vegetation grew thicker and I couldn't see through it.

Instead I kept peering into it, slowly shifting my feet, wincing at my inability to move quietly. My steps were like seismic events despite my attempted stealth, my breath had turned foul, and sweat poured like a river down my back. If one of my infinitely more sensible colleagues had asked me at that point why I was still moving forward, and why had I not noticed the tracks all around me, I may not have given the honest answer, which was that I craved interaction with animals so deeply that I didn't mind if I came out the other end of it (or them).

So I clumsily quaked my way forward, falsely confident that I would see anything before it was too late, when a bush beside me erupted.

With no ceremony three young warthogs had charged out from the guarri bush they had been sitting under, and took off down the road, their tails held jauntily upright. I leaped high enough to be afraid of the landing, and gave a yelp that would have impressed no one.

As my feet touched dirt again I cursed the pigs for scaring me so badly, then immediately forgave them as I had a premonition of something bad about to happen. The lions must be hiding somewhere in the bushes ahead, and the unknowing warthogs would be running right at them.

Within yards the first pig was rugby-tackled by a lioness. It gave a heartbreaking squeal as it was taken down. The next pig turned just in time to avoid a swiping paw and accelerated with astonishing power into a thicket, a lioness diving in behind it. The third little pig spotted yet another lion and swerved, its course taking it down the road edge, back toward me. As quick as it might be, it couldn't beat a lion in a flat sprint, and would have served itself best by heading into dense vegetation where the lion's bulk would slow it down. But this pig did one of the smartest things I had even seen an animal do, and swerved again, into the middle of the dirt road, and charged.

Straight at me.

It missed my shins by inches, and sped off. I stayed stock still as the lion that had been pursuing it now had a new target. I had hoped that she would be so intent on her prey that she'd ignore me, or by some miracle not notice me at all, but the pig had been correct and she was forced to choose between bacon or man-meat. She hauled up, her paws dragging and spraying a wave of dirt onto me, but I didn't dare to even blink at the dust as it hit.

We stood a few yards apart, measuring each other's intent, and weighing our options. I couldn't outrun her, and if I tried what the second pig had done and dived into the bush my greater size would leave my backside hanging out, and I would end up being hastily chewed on. The only option was to stand my ground.

4

The lion, however, had to choose between three things: chase the pig, which was probably long gone; run back to her sister and squabble over the food she'd caught; or eat me instead.

She took an aggressive step forward, spitting a gruff cough from her throat. It was a test. If I ran, she would know I was weak, but while I stood my ground she'd continue to feel doubt as to whether I had some strength that could leave her injured. I gave a small flinch, but stayed cemented to the road.

I wondered why she wasn't going back to the first pig. I knew enough about lions to understand that if food was available they would very rarely pass it up, particularly if any other options required hard work.

Then I remembered the second little pig, the one that had dived into the bush, and the lion that had followed. I hadn't heard a squeal, maybe missing the sound in the heat of the moment— but what if that pig had also run past me as the third had done, and right now, somewhere behind me there was a lion stalking, on the road that I had only seconds before been so confidently walking down? Was I being set up? Was the lion I faced seeing if she could distract me while her sister crept up from behind?

My eyes flickered to the side, trying to rotate and straining at the muscles that held them. The lion caught the movement and her muscles tensed, flexing, ready to fire her two-hundred-pound bulk at the first sign of weakness.

"Don't look behind you," I thought to myself, though my skin was crawling with ants.

There was a snarl, and the lion in front of me unfurled, making her decision. She raced back to the already dead warthog, and with a growl tore into the meat, wrestling with her sister over pieces of flesh.

I looked behind me. The road was empty, except for tracks that now appeared blindingly obvious to me—lions, one sole human fool walking amongst them, and in the other direction desperate scampering hoof marks, drawn long in the sand as a warthog ran for its life.

Edging away as cautiously as I could, still unaware where the third lioness was, not knowing which way to turn, the solution occurred to me. I would test my very rational fear of lions against my somewhat irrational fear of heights. I tried to remember what someone had once told me: "You're not really afraid of heights. It's the ground that'll kill you."

Maintaining slow pirouettes as I went, hoping to spot the third lioness if she was stalking me, I wound the thirty or so long yards to the tower. Sure that as soon as I started to climb I would be leapt upon, I powered my way up. Up past my head height, up past the rung where the frog remained impassively on his perch, up to the platform, and with a degree of elation overriding my desperation, further, through the barely shoulder-width cage and higher, all the way to the top, in time to watch the third lioness emerge from some bushes where she had watched me and join the fray of her sisters as they finished off the first little pig.

The adrenaline that had let me climb the tower without pause or waver still flooded my muscles, and with nothing useful for them left to do they set to shivering, despite the day's heat. The tower vibrated with me, my brain rattled in its pan, and I felt a mixture of emotions. I felt guilt that it was my actions that had led to the little pig's premature death. I felt pride at having climbed the tower. I felt the incomparable rush that comes from having been so close to a violent death and making it out alive. While I doubted that I had cured my fear of heights, I had a feeling that my fear of the job might be misplaced. Maybe, just maybe, I was going to be okay at this.

Now all I had to do was get back down.

STAY CALM, BUT MOVE FAST

Safari guides are notoriously bad drivers. We are impressive when facing tire-suckingly deep mud or casually steering through seemingly impassable boulders. But since most safari drives are conducted at a pace that would bore a tortoise, outside of the bush we tend to think that twenty miles an hour is really rocketing. We are easily distracted by the things we may not usually see in our work life. Attractive women, for example. Out of habit we tend to swerve across, or even off the road for a better look, just as we would do in the bush. We are dreadful at parking, too, it being a skill as easily shed as algebra is after graduation.

In this group of underachievers, I was a born dunce. My mechanical lexicon is limited to words like "wheel" and "seat," and I have a far greater talent for breaking vehicles than fixing them.

The guides I worked with, who were training me to join their ranks, all seemed born with at least a modicum of mechanical knowledge and a stoic ingenuity, rebuilding radiators from old toilet parts and casually saying things like "the diff is shot," and clearly knowing whatever the hell that means.

For the safety of the tourists whom I would soon be leading on safari, for the sake of the vehicles, and as a kind concession to me, the owners of the camp where I was working agreed to send me into the closest town, called Hazyview, for a driving course, the last piece of my yearlong guide training before I could begin my new career.

The vehicle we used to drive the six-hour round-trip to

shops and back was painted with gaudy black and white stripes, to reflect our camp's name of Idube, the local name for zebra.

I passed through Hazyview, and followed the road to Nelspruit, but before I reached there I saw the turnoff I needed, and took the Zebramobile down a corrugated track, and swung onto a property where barking dogs of indeterminate breed greeted me loudly.

The dogs were shushed and dismissed by two smiling and eager young fellows, probably only a few years older than my twenty-one years. They quickly ran me through what we would be doing on the course, before giving me the wheel of a Land Rover and explaining that what we did next would probably frighten me.

It did.

With a brief promise that the car could tip sideways to forty-five degrees before toppling over, which was far steeper than you'd think, we started along a rock face at an angle that to me was just a little rude. My head banged into the side window before my neck remembered its job and held it steady. Dirt loomed just past my right ear, and I blipped the throttle a little harder, trying to get this bit over with.

"Not scared, huh?" the instructor said, misinterpreting my hastening the finish for a gung-ho attitude that I've never possessed with driving, or pretty much anything except facing animals.

As the instructor now thought that I was up for any challenge, he gave me one. After piloting the vehicle over some rough logs that were strapped together, straddling a river, we ended at the top of a rocky ridge, with a smooth lip that curved gracefully to a near-vertical drop. The view was lovely, the greens and yellows of banana palms prominent, punctuated by blue bags hanging over the bunches of fruit to deter thieving monkeys. I could have stayed there for hours, but the instructor wanted me to drive off the cliff.

"What?" I said, sure he must be mentally impaired.

But over we went, the gears set in low range, seat belts on to stop us from tumbling out through the windshield. It wasn't that far a drop, but enough for my phobia to kick in, and I pressed back into my seat, as if I could burrow through and escape this lunacy. My body parts are never something I have had much control over, and now my ears tried to move to the back of my head out of fear, drawing my mouth into a rictus. Again, this was misinterpreted as a smile, and the instructor who had started the day hesitantly was now fully enthused, and said, "Man, you are going to just love Miss Piggy."

I doubted it, but at least she wasn't up high.

Miss Piggy was a mud pool that was used to test not whether a driver could avoid getting stuck, but to practice how to get out once he or she was. It was an axle-deep gloop, at the base of a small valley, stinking of years of agricultural runoff, a mixture of manure and rotten banana that made me crave gum boots.

Instead, I was given a second vehicle, an unsuspecting and less expensive Toyota Hilux, and told to plow it into the muck. Like all young fellows I had seen too many movies where something declared impossible is achieved, and the hero steps from his chariot with an air suggesting that he knew all along he'd succeed. I knew the aim was for me to get stuck, but I fantasized about sailing through, emerging on the other side and asking flippantly, "So where's this place that no one has ever driven through?"

I made it about three feet in and all four wheels spun furiously, digging me deep, deep down. Both instructors had watched from the Land Rover, and emerged chuckling. "That's the short-est distance anyone has ever gone," they snorted a bit, "We'll have to mark it as a record."

"Thanks," I replied, trying to muster some pride but know-ing it was in the mud with the car's wheels.

Since the vehicle wasn't where it would normally end up, the usual method of jacking it up wheel by wheel and placing logs underneath them wouldn't work, as the expanse of mud still in front would take forever to traverse. Instead we would use a high-lift jack to raise the entire front end, and once elevated push it off the jack so it fell a few feet sideways. We'd repeat at the back end, then again the front, slowly walking it to firmer ground.

"Easy," I announced, having already helped the others back at camp many times with the heavy, skeletal-looking jacks as they changed their regularly punctured tires. I mus-cled the jack from its bracket, and as always the deadly heavy fulcrum clattered to the base, swinging the apparatus on an arc that narrowly missed my shins. Using a wide base plate, it was seated under the push bars that protected the headlights, and I started cranking, hard work despite the leverage of the long handle.

It was with the greatest reluctance that the mud gave up its prize, and with a roaring squelch the tires came free. I wiped glop from my eye, and signaled to the instructors that it was ready for the shove. They started moving to the side of the car. I suddenly thought I should check what the vehicle would land on and peered around the edge of the car, just as it was given a push.

Most of a utility vehicle's mass is at the front—its engine, its heavy nudge bars, the electronics and starter motor—and it was this mass that had made it so difficult for me to raise it from the mud. It was this same mass now that was dropping, still on the jack, toward me.

The jack handle, at its full arc with all that weight, was swinging like a propeller blade, and hit me in the hairline above my right temple.

The impact was more sound than sensation, a brain-trembling *klonnnnng!* It was a cartoonish noise inside my head that didn't deserve to be taken seriously. I was knocked down, but sprang back up in the way your body demands when it is being assaulted.

"Are you okay?" one of the instructors asked.

"Sure," I said, my voice sounding distant to me, as if I had been granted the gift of ventriloquism.

"Man, you're bleeding," the other instructor said quietly, a touch of awe in his voice. He didn't have to tell me, though, because I could already see it. My head is a scarred old place, and I know how much the area exsanguinates. After the violence of the blow I had expected to be blinded in blood, but my vision stayed clear, clear enough to see a red geyser spouting like a poor special effect in front of me.

"Okay, who knows first aid?" I asked, since so far we had just all stood around as if my spouting head was a new water feature to be admired.

The two instructors looked at each other, back at me, then back at each other. Throughout the day I'd developed the impression that like me they were just getting started in their industry, and while competent in their field they carried a nervousness suggestive that they weren't ready for a disaster. Such as a client bleeding arterially.

They were still swinging their heads, like the clowns at a funfair whose mouths you pop balls into. A strange feeling of calm came over me. While I am never one to handle a social situation with aplomb, and have eyes that water at any human confrontation, I enjoy crises. A lot. Give me fires, give me floods, give me blood, and I am in my element. It is the only time that I don't have the pervasive nagging in my head that I am still a boy, and become an adult.

"Okay, stay calm, but move fast. This is an emergency." They stopped their head swings and now started nodding metronomically in a way that would have been entertaining if I wasn't bleeding to death. "You're going to have to put a compression bandage around my head, but tight, okay, so tight I won't be able to give instructions." They carried on nodding, but then one broke away and grabbed a first-aid kit from the vehicle that wasn't stuck.

"Tell me we don't have to go back up that cliff to get out of here . . . please?" I felt the first tinge of fear.

"No," the instructor said, and then more confidently, "No. We can go around the Pig and . . . " he carried on, glad to be back into route planning and away from patient care. I was woozy, but also knew that staying upright was the best way to slow the blood flow to my head, and therefore from leaking out of it. I had taken some relevant courses a few years previously, when I had taken a job as a pleasure cruise deckhand after abruptly leaving home and school. In that job I had regularly been faced with crushed toes, broken fingers, and other injuries resulting from the combination of alcohol, moving dance floors, and white people.

I explained to them that the amount of blood I was losing might mean that I would pass out, but above all they needed to get me to a doctor as soon as possible. Hazyview was closest, so they said they'd aim for that. This was not a place or time where cell phones existed, so there was no calling ahead to see if the surgery was closed, something not unusual even on a weekday if there had been a drunken brawl on a farm somewhere that the doctor needed to attend to.

They bandaged me tight, loops passing from under my chin, over the top of my head, needlessly swaddling my right eye, but I wanted to encourage the guys so I said nothing.

As we drove past Miss Piggy, through narrow gaps in banana palms, back over the log bridge that for many was a utility, not a challenge, I started to worry. I wasn't bothered that I might bleed to death, but more about what would happen if I didn't. From the age of four to sixteen I had played rugby, a game I am spectacularly bad at. This combined with my clumsiness meant I had suffered many spectacular concussions, sometimes so jarring that I had hallucinated, including one occasion where mid-game I became convinced that I was a sixteenth-century Japanese parasol salesman and tried to get players from each team to purchase my wares (later I'd had to explain to my team that I wasn't nuts, but had just read a book about the era in Japan—but the umbrella aspect still baffles me). No matter how entertaining these incidents, they were always followed by a paralyzing migraine. This is what concerned me the most as we drove to the doctor's, as I sat in his room, as I wilted in and out of consciousness, while he roughly shaved an unfashionably large chunk of my head, and while he stitched it up with red thread that blended nicely with a crust that was already forming on my scalp.

The doctor explained that the artery above my right eye had been crushed so completely that it could not be reconnected. Instead he had just tied off its end. I imagined it had been delivering blood somewhere important, but the doctor didn't seem concerned by this. I was too distracted by a reflection of myself, my new hairstyle making me look like a demented cockatoo, to be worried about long-term effects either. This stylish coif was soon swaddled in a turban of bandages, neater than the instructors had done but no more flattering, bulging out so my head looked like that of an alien from a fifties sci-fi flick.

The second instructor had tailed us in the Zebramobile, and I was now tentatively offered the keys and asked if I'd be all right getting back to the bush. The black and white stripes wavered as I looked at them, as if through a heat haze.

"Sure," I said, not wanting to stay the night and bleed on a stranger's sheets. I was also concerned that once the concussion took hold I would try to sell them something. Bananas maybe, inspired by the local vendors.

It was a three-hour drive back to camp, and I wanted to be there before the full migraine rendered me immobile and speechless. It was wildly irresponsible of me to drive, and I should have known better, but with liters of blood missing, a slowdown in the nutrient flow to my brain, and the feeling of immortality common to youth I hopped into the Zebra, popped its tiny engine into life, and set off.

I left Hazyview, passed the golf club whose lawns were occasionally overrun by hippos, passed the hand-painted signs advertising witch-doctor services, tire repairs, communion with God, newly hatched chickens, shebeens, tomatoes, and wooden crafted giraffes. I turned from the tar road and immediately was in the rural area that bordered the Kruger National Park. I swept through, waving to the village children, smiled knowingly at the men who stood holding shovels and dripping with sweat, calling for tips for their voluntary road repair (which they would dig up again the next day to retain their employment). Finally I was at the reserve gates. The gate guard asked for money, as he always did, even though he knew the Zebramobile was given free passage. Maybe he thought I was new enough, or that the head injury was severe enough that I'd hand over cash. I laughed at him, glad that I could laugh still yet wondering when my head would erupt with pain.

I drove on, weaving to avoid a puff adder as it made its sluggish way across the road, even in my distress keeping my eyes open in the hope of spotting something interesting, and took the turn to the camp too fast, hitting a lip on the track hard and bouncing the Zebramobile on and off its wheels like a rocking horse. A flare of pain lit behind my forehead and I gripped the wheel, wanting only to drive the last few miles to camp where I would be comfortable and safe in my tent. I suddenly regretted not having stayed in Hazyview, whether or not I would have felt awkward doing so, because it would be downright foolish and possibly dangerous sitting out here in the bush for a night if nobody thought to look for me.

The pain subsided to a random blinking, and soon I pulled into the back of camp. The camp manager, a dry-humored man named Devlin, burst out laughing at my turban, but the girls I worked with were kinder. I said I was going straight to bed before I became a menace, or offered them an umbrella, at which they all just looked at me blankly.

I lay there for a few hours, aware of every twinge and a new tightness to my scalp. It occurred to me that the migraines I'd had in the past probably indicated the death of thousands of brain cells, and at least showed that I had some functioning ones left. I theorized that the lack of agony might be due to a dearth of living matter between my ears.

I hoped my theory was incorrect, because I drifted off to a painless sleep and woke feeling just fine, and approached Devlin. "So, I've driven off a cliff. Am I ready to take out tourists yet?"

"Is your brain damaged?"

"I think so," I replied honestly.

"Well in that case, you're not a perfect candidate to be given a rifle, a vehicle, and a bunch of tourists." He paused, and my heart sank. "But brain damage isn't the worst thing suffered by someone out here, so why the hell not." Then he spoke the most exciting words I had ever heard. "You're a safari guide now."

TITUS AND THE CHAMELEONS

No matter how much I strained, I could not see the bloody leopard. I wasn't prepared to admit this to the tourists, though. My eyeballs felt coarse from the unblinking intensity with which I was peering, aiming in the direction that Titus had indicated as he casually uttered the magic word "*Ingwe*." In almost every language in Southern Africa this meant leopard, the most elusive of the large predators.

Of the many physiological flaws that I was aware of, becoming a guide had made me particularly aware that my senses were a tad wonky. My ears sent the wrong messages to my brain constantly, so I never knew where sound came from, and I considered myself legally nose-deaf, due to a deviated septum that gave me almost no sense of smell. But my eyesight was fine, better than average even, or at least that is what I had always thought. Yet Titus was casually cleaning under one of his nails with a thorn he had plucked from an acacia, as if the location of the leopard was so obvious that it would be rude for him to point it out more specifically.

Yet specifics would have thrilled me. I was beginning to feel like the Helen Keller of safari guides, barely able to communicate what I knew, and unable to see or hear that which I was meant to show.

"So Peter, is it in that tree with the green leaves, or the other one?" Now the tourists were befuddling me. All the bloody trees had green leaves. This man had asked, and not in a kindly way, which pre-school had let me out for the day when I'd introduced myself. My youth had made the few tourists I had led on safari immediately nervous, and this group was no different. This was the first drive I had with these tourists, and I was keen on establishing credibility quickly, but could feel it slipping from my grasp.

"Yes," I replied, not answering his query at all but hopefully stalling him for a moment, while I looked for the slightest flick of a tail tip, the twitch of a whisker, the flap of a leaf fanned by leopard's breath. None came, and I cursed myself for having announced Titus's discovery before I'd located it myself.

Titus sat on a custom seat at the very front of the vehicle, on the left-hand side of the hood. This allowed him to scan the road for spoor as we drove, and gave him a more elevated perch than my sunken driver's seat. Perhaps it was the height that let him see the leopard, I thought, and slid up from my seat to sit on the vehicle's side, on the narrow sill from which a window would emerge in a regular car.

My movement caught the leopard's attention, and I got the tail twitch I had been hoping for.

"Wow," I said, unable to mask my shock. The leopard wasn't in the tree with green leaves, whichever one the tourist had meant, but so far from the road that with the naked eye I could barely make it out. Even through my binoculars it was far from filling the field of vision, and I said, "Wow," again, then added, "Great spot, Tussy."

Titus (or Tussy as he was sometimes called) and I worked well together, as I was willing to learn from him and take his advice when choosing a direction. We communicated with sign language, his few words of English, my few of Shangaan, and a cocktail of a language called Fanagalo, invented for South Africa's mine workers, an African Esperanto with wonderfully onomatopoeic words like "Shtoo-Toot" for a motorbike and "Gunda-Gunda" for a tractor.

"Ya, *umfo*, nice!" Titus replied, using Afrikaans for yes, Shangaan for brother, and English for the rest.

I turned the vehicle off the road and started trundling it toward the reposing leopard, which was regally sitting at the base of a tree. The tree, I was forced to note, had reddish leaves.

"How did he see that? Is it wearing some kind of tracking collar?" green-leaf man asked. The leopard quite clearly was not, and these sorts of questions were already frustrating.

"Not that I can tell," I piped up, wanting to defend Tussy. "Must have just been talent."

And talent it was. Titus could spot things around corners, I was convinced of it. I have worked with a small few people as good as him over the years, but none better. His ability was exemplified by a trick that he did once the sun had set, and we carried on with our drives using spotlights to follow nocturnal creatures. He had a thorough methodology with his light, sweeping from side to side, covering different levels of foliage and on every third sweep checking the road for animal tracks or the reflection of eyes, his head following the beam like a sniper behind his weapon.

The bright flash of a lion's eye was no challenge to see, but Titus would on occasion start shaking the light up and down, indicating to me that he had seen something worth stopping for. The light would steady on a bush, or tree branch.

"*Lumfaan,*" was all he needed to say for me to know that I had a challenge. I would immediately get my binoculars out and peer at the leaves, bleached by the light, for the shape of a chameleon. To spot such a thing, famous for being hard to see, and to do it at night was staggeringly impressive.

Tourists, if they managed to identify this most famous exponent of camouflage, would be awestruck, and convinced that Titus had some mystical powers.

They were not far from the mark, as his sideline interest was in witch-doctoring, particularly poisons and hallucinogens. In fact, earlier that day I'd sat down with Titus for the sort of chat I enjoyed in Africa, using drawings in the sand where I lacked the words to express myself, exaggerated facial expressions for humor, and a hodgepodge of terminology from whatever common vocabularies we might have.

He pulled some hard-looking seeds from his pockets, pecan-sized nuts shaped like an egg that had been laid on its side and compressed. At the larger end there were three conspicuous eyes, and Titus took an implement from his other pocket and started cracking these open. I knew from the books that I had been poring over that these were marula nuts, left over from the tasty marula fruits that had been around in February. These fruits were relished by monkeys, birds, and elephants in the trees, and warthogs and porcupines when they fell.

Some fibers from the fruit still clung to parts of the seed pod, and Titus occasionally blew at these as we chatted, finally prising open an eye to reveal a seed inside. I had read that these seeds were highly nutritious, with oil so rich that they could be lit and would burn like a candle. They were delicious, somewhere between walnuts and well-cooked mushrooms, and between appreciative chews I asked, "Titus, how do you see the chameleons?"

He chuckled, waggled a finger at me, and dug into another nut.

"Come on, how?"

He kept digging, as if all his concentration was required. I tried drawing a chameleon in the sand, but my artistic ability had peaked at age two and it looked more like a turd dropped from on high.

20

"*Lumfaan?*" Titus asked, pointing at my doodle. Reluctantly, I acknowledged, that yes, I had intended the scrawl to resemble a chameleon. Titus's already large smile became a dazzle of teeth as his chuckle turned to outright laughter. He dropped his nuts, slapped his thigh, and the tool fell from his hand. Then a pitying look came over his face, the only time I recall ever seeing him when his enormous teeth weren't on display.

"White," he said simply, and I thought that as so often happened in South Africa the conversation was about to turn to race, and I had no idea why. Then he pointed at my splotch, and quickly spread his fingers, before just as quickly closing them again. The pale undersides of his dark hands had made a white starburst, and I got it. The chameleons looked white at just the right angle from the spotlight, just as some animals' eyes reflected different colors depending on the angle the beam reached them. I was thrilled with this discovery, and couldn't wait to try it out.

Then something else dawned on me. "Titus, you found these marula nuts lying around in the bush, didn't you?"

"*Yebo.*"

"So you've been sitting there, smiling, and feeding me warthog droppings?"

He just grinned at me, then burst out laughing again, before popping some more seeds into his mouth. While the thought of eating something that had passed a warthog's bowels might perturb most, I was not overly fazed. My philosophy has always been to try any food on the condition that someone before me has eaten it, and lived. But the glee Titus was taking from my imagined discomfort meant that an unwritten masculine rite had begun, the sort that made wildebeest butt heads. I simply had to get him back, and hoped it would happen that evening.

◉

The opportunity wouldn't come with this leopard we were watching, though. It wasn't interested in us, or moving, so we pushed on to a rocky hill nearby, locally known as a *kopje*. I took out a basket so the tourists had drinks to watch the sundown with, made sure they were comfortable, and went over to Titus. He was having his customary sweet fizzy drink while I downed a bottled water, craving something stronger.

"Great spot, Tussy, nice sighting."

"Ya, *umfo*. Nice!" He grinned, knowing that I was generous in splitting the tips tourists gave me, whether he found leopards or not, and that I often bought him a beer after a successful drive.

Soon I rounded up the tourists, and we drove off after I had explained that not all eyes we saw would belong to lions, and to not feel the need to point out every cluster of bright spots they saw, as that would be herds of impala and we wouldn't shine on them.

We had barely set off when the light jiggled. I slowed, not sure if Titus had seen something or if it was merely the light bouncing from my erratic driving. The light shook more vigorously, so I slowed, trying to catch the flash of white that Titus had told me about.

But it was a gorgeous little white-faced owl, glaring angrily at us for a few perfect moments before flying off to terrorize the mice within the reserve.

"Well spotted, Tussy," the irritating man said, bothering me by using a nickname he hadn't been granted permission to employ. Getting desperate to show that I could do something more than push an accelerator and steer, I leaned forward in my seat, and craned my neck to full extension, as if somehow I'd see animals sooner by being a few inches forward.

22

I tracked the spotlight, and almost shouted "Eyes!" a few times before realizing it was just impala. Then I jammed on the brakes. Titus gave a panicky grab at one of the handrails beside his seat, steadied himself, and looked back at me to see why I had come so close to throwing him off the vehicle. I was trying to play cool, but a grin that would have made Titus proud was spreading from ear to ear.

"Chameleon," I announced to the tourists as casually as I could.

Titus's spotlight went berserk, rapidly scanning every tree branch, every bush, even patches of the open night sky, perhaps thinking I was just incompetent enough to think lizards could fly. It was like Dresden in World War Two.

"Where?" one of the tourists asked.

I popped my door open, slid from my seat, and took a casual step to the right. Titus lit me up as if finding an enemy bomber. I stopped only a pace away from his feet, leaned down, and plucked a grass stem from beside the road.

The only place not covered by Titus's sweeps were the exact places hit by the edge of the headlight beams, and in these I had seen the flash Titus told me of, a baby chameleon that didn't even cover my palm when I showed it to the tourists, still sitting on the grass stem it had been clutching when I saw it.

"Wow, Peter, that's amazing." It was my nemesis the tourist, now praising me, "You've got great eyes!"

"Thanks," I said, and smiled at Tussy, as if I was about to explain that it was he who had taught me how to do this trick, but said nothing.

"Just talent, I guess," the tourist echoed what I'd said earlier, then bellowed, "Hey Titus, how come you didn't see that?"

Titus didn't answer, instead turning his back and hunching over the light, sulking.

I put the chameleon back where I had found it, its eye swiveling to watch me as I walked away and hopped happily back into my seat. As soon as we set off, Titus sat back upright. Professionalism, I thought. Clearly not a man to brood. He scanned left with his light, at head height, swinging the beam around to the right. All the way around, right into my eyes.

The beam went left again, higher this time, but dipped on the way back, and swung into my eyes.

It was a miracle we made it home, because I really was a blind guide by the time we got there. I fumbled in the darkness when we arrived in camp, my startled retinas having a rough time adjusting to the mild lighting of the camp. I sought out Titus, and said, "Truce?" I saw no teeth, surely the brightest thing in the region, and thought maybe he didn't know the word. "Peace?"

He laughed, "Ya, *umfo!* Nice! Peace!"

24

LIGHTS AT NIGHT

I have always liked driving at night . . . your thoughts accompanied by nothing but a growl from the engine, the swish of tires on the road, punctuated by the occasional pop as a piece of gravel is shot from underneath, pinging musically against the underside of the vehicle on its way.

There was no romance, though, in the drive I took to collect paperwork from our reserve's Gothic wooden gate early one night. With no roof on the car, the wind was bitingly cold, numbing my lips, and making my fingers ache. I resented the broken latches on the windshield, which lay down slovenly against the front hood, offering no protection against the cold night air.

My shoulders were hunched to prevent any wind from sliding in under my collar, meaning that I couldn't scan from side to side, like you should when driving in the bush. There might be elephants there, or rhinos, ready to rampage out and stomp the buzzing tin box I rode in to pieces. A hippo this far from the river was unlikely, but I knew that luck came in two flavors and maybe some cranky mammal was just where I wasn't looking, lurking like a mugger. My melodramatic thoughts were a symptom of the mind, doing its utmost to distract me from the one thing that was really bothering me.

There were lights in the sky, not like any helicopter or plane I had ever seen, coming closer.

I'd noticed it as soon as I had hit the long, relatively straight "main" road we used to get to the gate. My eyes were drawn along the ribbon of dirt to a gap in the trees, and up to the stars that shone brighter than in any city. Amongst them was something

25

wrong, that made me do a cartoonish double-take, letting a sneaky breeze slip into my shirt. I shuddered at the cold, then once more in reaction to what I was seeing.

A string of round lights, like linked Chinese lanterns, hung in the sky straight ahead. I couldn't gauge their distance, or their velocity, or even if they were moving at all. My eyes were spending more time looking at the sky than at the road, convinced the lights were inexorably drawing closer, maybe even subtly altering course to come at me.

Stop it, I insisted to myself twice, slightly embarrassed. I don't consider myself a fanciful person, and while I had read plenty of science fiction when I was younger, now I violently resisted the idea that what I was looking at was piloted by aliens.

Yet it was certainly not any normal aircraft, nor something uncommon but explicable like an airship. Was it coming closer? It was so hard to tell as until now I had resolutely kept driving, refusing to bow to silly fears.

I braked to a stop, and with some reluctance switched off the engine, letting the silence crash in. Whatever was in the sky made no noise, and only the intrusion of an owl's call made me feel like I was still on a familiar planet.

Looking at the lights now, it didn't seem they were moving at all, certainly not hunting me. I giggled a bit for letting foolishness overtake me. There was a rational explanation to this, there had to be. Mustering bravado from somewhere I yanked the key to the right to start the engine again. It just whirred, and stopped.

"No way!" I exclaimed. I'd seen enough movies to know what happened next. The lights would shoot a beam onto me, then I'd be drawn up into a craft where large-headed aliens with black almond eyes would perform experiments on my anus.

Were the lights brighter now? I giggled again, the sound loud enough to spook myself and yet still trigger some more hysteria. I yanked the key once more, and the engine started perfectly normally, except I'd taken my foot off the clutch so it stalled.

"Bet it doesn't go this time," I said to myself, yet it did, and I puttered along the track, watching the lights too much and not seeing bumps in the road that made my teeth clack violently. I hoped they weren't tortoises.

The mechanical sound of the engine gave me a sense of security, but my sparse body hair was still raised into gooseflesh, which I couldn't blame on the night air. I felt lonely, which gave me an idea. In movies nobody got kidnapped while they were talking to someone, so I grabbed the radio mike and called the camp.

"Base base base, come in," and waited. "Base base base, come in," and waited some more. "Idube Idube Idube, come in for Peter," but they didn't come in. I'd seen this movie. Everyone in the world had been kidnapped by aliens, except me, and now I was going to be alone for the rest of my life.

Except for hyenas, I thought, as one loped across my head-light beams. If only one animal was going to be left behind with me, couldn't it have been cuter? Or at least something that tasted good?

"Go, Young Takker," burst Devlin's voice from the radio, using his standard address for me.

"Hey Dev, I'm almost at Newington Gate, and just wondered if you can step outside the office for a second, look at the sky to the, um, hang on, north, and tell me what you see?" I didn't want to lead him with information in case I was merely hallucinating, or if this was a temporary result of my recent head injury.

"I see the sky, you moron. Stop wasting my time," Devlin spoke to everyone like that, doing his utmost to disguise that he was actually a very generous person.

"Come on Dev, just take a quick look, please,"

There was silence at the other end as I moved ahead, adding to the usual danger of my driving by staring at the sky and clutching a radio mike in one hand, operating the gears with the other and steering with my legs when I had to.

"Nope," came Devlin's voice, "nothing there. Have you been drinking?"

I was distraught. The lights were perfectly clear to me, brighter than anything else in the sky. If Devlin couldn't see them, then there was only one conclusion. I'd gone nuts.

I was pondering my insanity and the state African asylums would be maintained in when my radio crackled back to life. "Peter, it's Melanie here, Devlin's just being a pig, we can all see the lights. What are they?"

"We can see them too," came a different voice, which I recognized as the manager of another camp in the reserve. More voices joined in, and soon the radio was alive with a comforting chatter as people throughout our little bush outpost theorized and postulated as to what could be making the phenomenon, whether it was moving or stationary, or even if this heralded some biblically predicted Armageddon. After this last suggestion, we all maintained an embarrassed silence on the radio before someone made the sound of a game show's "fail" buzzer, and the group babbled on to each other.

I watched the lights all the way to the gate. The night watchman was engaged in the traditional activity of every night watchman that I ever met in Africa, which involved snoring violently enough to vibrate the shack that he sat in. After some rousing he peered angrily at me, clearly preferring slumber to duty, and crankily thrust me the papers. Wanting to cheer him up, I said, "*Boya umfo*," and he reluctantly followed me outside.

He exited with his back to the lights, and I made a gesture with my fingers that he should turn around. He did, looked casually at the lights, smacked his lips with disinterest, farted violently, and went back into his hut. He was snoring again by the time I'd finished holding my breath and started the drive back to camp. Clearly if the lights weren't a threat, and weren't offering him anything of value to the gate guard, they were nothing worth commenting on. At least not verbally.

Trying to be sensible, and even brave, I drove back without looking behind me too often. The lights weren't moving, though the debate on the radio still raged as to whether they were pulsing or not.

Back in camp I rushed to the *boma* where we ate our meals, eager to hear more ideas as to what the U.F.O. could be, but conversation had moved on. The tourists had seen lions that day, and hippos, a rhino, warthogs, and antelope, things as rare to them in their city lives as lights at night were to us.

The next night I peered into the sky again, but the lights weren't there in the north, or any other point of the compass.

Almost a week later Iain came into the camp office with a three-day-old newspaper, quite fresh by our standards, and pointed out an article about a Russian satellite. One of its solar panels had broken, and for a while its angle to the sun and geosynchronous orbit had made for strange patterns of light in the sky in just the right part of the world. Our part.

It was gratifying to know what the lights were, though a part of me was saddened that the answer was not in the least bit exotic. At least, I thought to myself, I never had to befriend a hyena for company. Or find out how good they tasted.

Two Mpondo

Titus never moved in his car seat when lions walked right by him. He didn't flinch at leopards either. Once when an elephant chased us he gave me wild hand gestures as I reversed, indicating that I should plant my foot harder and get us out of there, but he stayed resolutely on his seat even though the elephant's looming tusks would have caught him first. A tracker like Titus could build his reputation on his ability to spot animals, also for following the marks they made to whatever place they might be hiding, but the real respect we paid him came from his sitting stoically while a lion rubbed its side against his shoes to relieve an itch, something I'd seen more than once.

There was only one animal I ever saw Titus shift for, and that was Uncle One Horn, the white rhinoceros. As was usual on one of our drives, Titus saw One Horn well before I did, even though the rhino loomed from the surrounding grassland like a boulder with ears. I slowed down and explained to the tourists on board that while this was an extraordinarily gentle example of the species, it was still a rhinoceros worthy of respect and as the vehicle approached it was prudent to keep voices low and movements to a minimum. He was, after all, a beast weighing more than six-and-a-half thousand pounds with serious armor.

At the sound of the diesel One Horn barely paused in his monotonous grazing. Instead, he just lifted his heavy head slightly to gaze myopically at us from the safe distance I had parked.

"Everyone calls this guy One Horn," I began.

"*Mpondo*," said Titus, who rarely interrupted me when I was speaking.

"Except Titus," I corrected myself, "who calls him One *Mpondo*," I added.

"What does that mean?" asked an American tourist.

"One Horn," I explained, hoping this didn't turn into a "Who's on first?" routine. "But I call him Uncle One Horn, because he is like an old uncle who might seem gruff but is really quite gentle." Nobody seemed moved by this information, or interested.

"He lost his back horn in a fight," I explained, "but the other guy lost the battle. One Horn is one of the strongest, most dominant males in the reserve."

"Should we be this close?" another American inquired.

"Sure," I said. I was in fact hoping the rhino would come closer, and had parked myself in the direction I had imagined he would move as he fed. He only displayed aggression to other male rhinos, and while he had the strength to casually tip us over should he desire, I felt safe with him. Of the animals I had come to know, he was a favorite.

Sure enough, he lumbered toward us with his next mouthful, his broad square lip cropping methodically at the stubbled grass in front of him, his pendulous head movements metronomic. Puffs of dust shot from his feet with each step, and the suspension springs creaked as all the tourists leaned further back in their seats, away from his formidable approach.

A beautiful silence descended as nobody dared speak, and I knew that all six tourists behind me would be holding their breath. I lived for these moments, not because I took any delight in the fear of others, but for being so close to a wild animal that was behaving just as he would do if we weren't there. I also knew that any fear the tourists felt now would be replaced by a life-affirming rush of adrenaline once he moved on, a residue of awe that could last for hours.

One Horn took a step closer, and the red-billed oxpeckers that had been perched on his flanks, cleaning the folds of skin around his thighs and genitals, flew off, calling raucously, not happy with how close he was drawing to the dangerous animals in the vehicle. One Horn paid them no heed, unconcerned by their warning that we might be predators, and came closer.

A bit too close. Titus, who was vastly more experienced than I was, gave me a hand gesture to suggest I briefly flick the engine into life, just enough to remind One Horn of our presence and make him take a step back. Rhinos have notoriously poor eyesight, but possess good hearing and a strong sense of smell, balanced by a tiny, tiny brain to retain information. Such as "Don't forget there is a Land Rover parked where normally there is just empty grassland."

I couldn't flick the engine, though, as I was mesmerized by his front horn, now angled toward me through the gap where my door had been removed. If his head jerked, I'd become a shish-kebab. The only sound was One Horn's nasal exhalations and his rhythmic chomping. I hoped the tourists, despite their fear, were enjoying this as much as I was.

He turned parallel to us, almost as long as the Land Rover, and grazed beside the vehicle. With a respect for geometry I didn't imagine he'd possess, he neatly turned the corner at the front of the vehicle and swung left, now moving toward Titus's feet. Titus raised his boots in a fluid motion, and near silently swiveled on his buttocks to place them on the bonnet. He was now facing me, with a thunderous look on his face only made worse as One Horn stopped grazing, and started scratching.

This was not the way a dog scratches, digging its toes into an ear or flank, but the rhino way. With skin up to two inches thick in places, they need to rub really hard against a surface to satisfy an itch, and even concrete-like termite mounds have shattered under their attention. One Horn had brushed past the grille that covered the Land Rover's radiator, found the sensation pleasant, and decided to give it a go. He leaned in, and began rubbing, his gentle exhalations turning to panting as he gave it some energy.

With startling violence the vehicle shook from side to side as he rubbed his mighty sides against it. The gauze placed over the grille to catch grass seeds ripped away, landing on One Horn's back, looking like the saddle for some elfin jockey. Next the grille itself tore, twanging as thick-gauge wire popped from the strain. The sharpened ends would be lethal for a person to use as relief, but One Horn gave a surprisingly human groan of pleasure as they touched him and with a disturbingly erotic huffing pushed harder against the wires, clearly in ecstasy. Maybe this itch had been there for a long time, maybe not, but he was deriving enormous satisfaction from relieving it. I just wasn't sure how much damage he was doing and whether we'd be able to drive away. I could possibly have stopped him by clinking something metal on metal, as this often worked to deter elephants, but was finding the whole scene quite amusing. Turning to the tourists, I saw nothing but broad smiles; one even had tears running down his face as he suppressed silent guffaws at One Horn's audible pleasure.

Titus, though, was clearly not finding the rodeo ride he was enduring at all entertaining. Never had I seen him leave his seat before, but now he slithered across the bonnet, coming precariously close to sliding onto One Horn's back before he could grip the windscreen frame.

One Horn's moaning now sounded like a caricature, his normal sedate dignity flung away. So absorbed was he that Titus's slither hadn't disturbed him, nor did he stop when Titus hauled himself over the dashboard and into the seat beside me.

I was laughing, but Titus shook his head at me.

"*Matata, umfo,*" he said, telling me this was not a laughing matter, but a problem, brother.

I immediately thought of the damage One Horn must have done, and as a guide how accountable I would be. I loved this new job of mine, passionately, and lived to have moments like I was currently having, and didn't want the opportunity taken away.

"Is the Landy broken?" I asked, not having the words in Titus's language yet to ask that.

"Not broken," Titus said. "*Mina booga* two *mpondo*" (I see two horns).

I immediately scanned the surrounding plain, sure that Titus was referring to a second rhino, and that he imagined we were about to become the meat in the sandwich of a titanic clash. But the plain held only our rocking vehicle, and the lone rhino.

Then I got it. "Oh," I said, then "Oh, bugger!" suddenly understanding there was another "horn" to worry about.

"Ya *umfo,*" Titus said, misunderstanding me. "*Booga!*" *Booga* means look, but I was at no angle to look for the second "horn" Titus had seen.

"One Horn *funa faga pagati*?" I asked, putting the question delicately.

"*Yebo,*" Titus said.

One Horn wanted to mate with us. *Now* I was ready to move the vehicle. I gave a click flick of the ignition, just one rotation of the starter motor, and One Horn snorted and backed away a pace, which was all the room I wanted or needed, so in reverse with the turbo whining I backed us away, bouncing out of divots and warthog scrapes in the ground before turning us away and moving to a safe distance.

"Did he get aggressive?" one of he tourists asked, a little rattled by our sudden ejection from the plain that I had given them no warning for.

I was young, a little shy about these matters, even though it was common to observe them in the natural world, so just answered, "he got . . . emotional."

"He seems to have an extra leg," an English lady said, her binoculars trained on him, her prim accent making the comment sound particularly hysterical to my juvenile ears, so I burst out laughing.

"Whole new meaning to horny," said the American, and the entire group erupted into laughter, even two Germans who'd said nothing so far.

"Was it Titus he liked, or the jeep?" someone asked.

"Don't know," I admitted, "but I doubt Titus is prepared to go back there to find out," and everyone was laughing again. "It would be a long experiment as well," I added, not realizing my double entendre, "because a rhino can mate for as long as two hours at a go."

Out on the plain One Horn stood, still holding his head high, poised expectantly.

"Two *Mpondo*," I said quietly to Titus, chuckling.

"*Mina saba, umfo*," Titus said, "I was afraid." In the months to come I would see a leopard charge him, a hippo run mouth agape and just miss his legs, and a lurking buffalo catch him unawares when he went for a pee, but I never heard him speak those words again.

LOLLIPOP

Every few months I'd hear of an incident in the bush that ended with a safari guide maimed or dead. Often the guide had taken a hearty leap over the thin line that separates bravery from stupidity, and tried something like plucking an elephant's tail hair. I'd usually mutter, "Well the bloody fool deserved it," but would, if pushed, confess to a sneaky desire to try the act myself.

Now I was sitting with four other guides on an inflated tractor tire tube, which was roughly lashed to another of its kind, and around and below me there were unknown numbers of crocodiles. The current was picking up, and for the first time in ages I was wearing underpants that were waterlogged and chafing mightily. I contemplated raising my concern that we were being indescribably stupid to raft a flooded, swollen river that carried the carcasses of drowned animals that were far better suited to this environment than we were. Then looking at my macho co-rafters, I decided against it. They were all bigger than I was and had no reason not to toss me to the crocs if I started whining.

I watched the Land Rover that we had arrived in as it drove off, Alpheus, the tracker, at the wheel. He wasn't excluded from our expedition based on race (he was black, and all five of us were varying degrees of sunburnt), but chose not to join us because he had a higher dose of common sense. His muttering had been audible as we explained that we planned to ride the tubes from the fenceline and see if we could make it all the way to the causeway by Inyanti Camp. Only some weeks later, after another event, would I wonder what he must have thought of us pursuing adventure in an environment that for him was purely to be endured, where for generations survival had been all that mattered. At the time I had happily ignored Alpheus's sensible protestations and, with testosterone overriding intellect, been the first on the raft.

We had the time to try this journey because our reserve was shut for the first time in living memory. The camps sat empty, the guides bored and restless. Rain had fallen for weeks, so relentlessly that most of our dirt tracks had disappeared and even our trusty four-wheel-drive vehicles spent more time stuck than moving. Tourists couldn't enter, and maintenance was pointless as the rain collapsed all structures and grew fine coatings of mold over everything else.

"Let's play poker!" Iain had first suggested, desperate to ease our boredom. It sounded fine, until we discovered no one knew the rules. So in lieu of sensible entertainment we hatched our plan to make a raft, and float down a raging river on it.

The reserve we worked in was liberally sprinkled with water holes, and bisected by the Sand River. The river was normally traversable year-round at two concrete causeways, which vehicles and animals used to cross, water sloshing around their ankles or axles. Crocodiles also used the causeway. They waited open-mouthed on the lower lip to catch fish as they tumbled over, or perhaps for safari guides like me who were poor drivers.

With no reason in the reserve to possess boats, there were none to be had, so we had been forced to design one. Apart from the two large tractor tubes and the twine that tied them, another length of cord trailed behind, lashed to a car's tube. This was the dinghy, the plan being if anyone fell off he could grab at it as he drifted past, and pull himself back onto the raft. It was a stupid, stupid idea, but we didn't let that bother us, and with two broom-handled machetes doubling as paddles and weapons, we were drifting down the Sand.

"Not sure if any of you have thought of this," I broached soon after we set off, "but using sharp implements as paddles in an inflatable raft might not work out for us in the long run." Not only were the blades honed, but they were tipped with a spike, perfect for hooking a wayward branch in normal usage but equally as good, I was sure, for turning our flimsy craft into something resembling a discarded condom.

I was paddling wide, sweeping strokes to avoid the rubber on which I sat on the left of the raft. I spied something swirling toward us in the current. "Log!" I called, and started jabbing furiously at it to stop it from colliding with us. My frenzied activity made our side of the craft bob nauseatingly, and spun the other tube around so it was now facing the danger.

Before setting out, we had spent some time figuring out how we would sit. There were five of us, so it wasn't an easy split between the two tubes, and choosing who got to hang their legs comfortably through the doughnut holes. Iain and Duncan were both well over six feet and muscularly built, so they took the less cramped quarters on the right-hand hull. Justin, Marius, and I were of similar height, but Justin had the build of the bouncer and bodyguard that he once had been, while Marius had the hefty farmer's build of his Afrikaner forebears. I was the lightest (yet somehow had the first shift paddling), and while everyone else had their legs through the doughnut hole in the middle of the tube, my knobbly limbs dangled temptingly over the outer edge. Now that my jabbing had created a spin, it exerted a centrifugal force, and I knew enough physics to understand that despite my firm clench, my buttocks simply could not get a firm enough grip to hold my body weight. I slid straight off the slick wet rubber and fell into the churning water.

"Bugger," I thought as my head went under. Immediately the strength of the current was violently evident. It tugged at my clothes, and almost wrenched the valuable machete clean out of my hands. I hauled back on it as I surfaced, and saw that I was swinging its blade toward Marius's leg. "Oops," I thought, halted its movement, and wondered why I was suddenly being dragged backwards. Before I could ponder just how many crocodiles there might be in this river, strong hands had hauled me back on board. I sheepishly stuck my legs into the crowded doughnut hole.

"Sorry for that," I said, while the rest avoided eye contact with me.

The log had been deflected during my aquatic expedition, and we now drifted on. The water was coffee brown, and foamed over half-seen rocks. "The hippos should be coming up soon," said Iain. "Glen saw them here earlier." In a rare sensible moment we had asked other guides where the resident pod of hippos was last seen, and in a unanimous decision said we would portage our raft around them. Territorial, bad tempered, and with long curving teeth that had no difficulty peeling open tin boats, a single hippo could make this a bad day for all of us.

"*Wheeee! Hoonk hoonk hoonk!*" The noise was loud, and far closer than I would have liked. Many animals will give you fair warning when you are coming too close to them, and a hippo was letting us know that we had been correct in our assessment of their location. We paddled madly for a bank, those without machetes using their hands for what little impetus they offered.

As frightened as I was, there was no time in my life that

I had been happier than at that moment, with animals ahead likely to kill me. This was why I lived in the bush, I thought. Taking tourists around could be fun, and there was real delight in seeing their faces light up at the antics of a lion cub or the tenderness shown by elephants, but this sort of adventure was what I had craved all my life. I paddled harder, wanting to ensure I lived long enough to get full value from this experience.

We made it to the bank with a chorus of snorts from the hippos, a small number of which had detached themselves and were now aggressively patrolling the section of river we had just left. Carrying the raft vertically, with me holding the dinghy like a bridal train, we followed a wide path cleared by elephants along the river until we were well past the hippos. I noticed that Marius wasn't wearing shoes. The rest of us had sandals on, and he was gingerly picking his way over the thorn-strewn ground, looking very uncomfortable.

"We should name our boat," I said.

"It's not a boat," Duncan said, matter-of-factly.

"Raft, then," I said.

"That's a good name," said Marius, and I couldn't tell if he was being sarcastic or not.

"I meant it's a raft, not a boat, or a ship. So let's call it *Lollipop*."

The look I received from all four fellow rafters suggested they thought I was mad, fruity, or both, and I wondered if maybe they didn't know the song. I also thought that breaking into the chorus of Shirley Temple's "Good Ship *Lollipop*" would do nothing to convince them that I was neither, so didn't bother explaining anymore.

We jumped back in, and I chose the best spot, where my feet were facing forward and would have some flex when they hit submerged rocks, something that had been extremely painful when they had been colliding sideways in the early stages of our journey.

"No more hippos!" Iain shouted, and whooped.

"Just crocs, what a relief," I thought, but whooped along as well. The sun was shining for the first time in weeks, we were moving fast, had no tourists to worry about, and were probably the first people to have ever rafted this river. I felt like an explorer. As the deep green papyrus and reeds on the banks whizzed by and the occasional startled heron or bittern squawked and flew out, I laughed for no reason, my laugh echoed by a snort.

Not from Duncan though, nor Justin, Marius, or Iain. It was another hippo.

"Single bull?" I asked, hopefully, thinking it might be a male that we could somehow scoot around using the dubious maneuverability of our craft. My question was answered when the snort was responded to with a series of nasal blasts ahead of us. It sounded like there were rather a lot of them.

"*Kak*," said Marius, which is Afrikaans for exactly what it sounds like.

The banks here on each side were thick with papyrus, and there didn't seem to be anywhere we could beach *Lollipop*. A small gap appeared on the northern bank, overhung with the branches from an ebony tree, and we paddled toward it with a desperation born of real fear.

A bull hippo aquaplaned toward us, terrifyingly fast. His head seemed as broad as the tractor tube. He dived, his bow wave the only evidence that he was still charging. Iain and Duncan slapped at the water with the flats of the blades to make sonic shocks underwater. He reappeared, closer, snorted again, and we all put renewed effort into making it to the beaching area.

We didn't make it. The beach went past, tantalizingly close, but despite momentous effort and a dangerous flurry of blades we were swept past it, on the edge of the river but straight toward the waiting pod of hippos. I thought of how skinny our submerged legs must look to the hippos and how contemptuously they could snap through them, and while I knew that, being vegetarians, they wouldn't consume us, the blood from their attack would attract creatures that would.

We halted abruptly and I jolted forward, wondering who had been grabbed, or what we had hit. It was Duncan. One of his long arms had shot out and grabbed a single cluster of reeds, which he grimly held by its razor-sharp leaves. Miraculously the vegetation had not torn loose, and he singlehandedly drew us to the wall of reeds where we could all assist, and hand-over-hand we dragged ourselves back to the beach.

This was not the sort of beach where you would set up a bright umbrella and expect cocktail service, but one littered with detritus from the river's path, gnarly with tree stumps and roots. It was serviced by a well-worn path made by generations of animals as they warily made their way down to drink. It was equally not a place that you would want to stand for too long, as it would no doubt be a favored spot for crocodiles to ambush their prey.

We immediately set about unlashing *Lollipop* so she could fit underneath the branches that grew over the path. We cautiously carried her through the brambles, a slow, strange, and reverent-looking procession as we did our utmost to avoid any thorns. The only sound was Marius's prolific swearing as these same thorns punctured his feet. I vaguely worried that the sounds of his distress might attract a predator, and pondered whether a lion would prefer to catch one of the larger guys for more meat, or me because I would seem the least equipped to put up a fight.

The path took us further inland, the river's roar growing fainter. The bush was too thick to hack our way through, so we pressed on along the path, heading farther north than any of us had been for a month.

Marius was relieved of carrying any part of *Lollipop*, as his mad hopping would surely swing her into a thorn, so the three parts were rotated between me, Justin, Iain, and Duncan. It was painfully slow and oppressively hot, but to take *Lollipop* through any other way would be fatal to her. We couldn't deflate her and squeeze her through, as it would take days of our combined lung power to reinflate her, and without her there was no way we could get back across the river.

"You know, we're the first people north of the river for months," Iain proclaimed, and seemed particularly delighted at our achievement.

"Except poachers," Duncan said flatly.

Unfortunately, he was right. The quality of light had changed, but it had nothing to do with the sun's angle. Strange glinting penetrated the brush, the reflections from hundreds, perhaps thousands, of snares set throughout the area. To add insult to injury, they were made from wire taken from the very fence meant to protect the wildlife.

"*Kak*," someone said softly, but this time not Marius.

"*Es a groot kak*," I added. Normally if I attempted to speak Afrikaans my mangled pronunciation and dubious grammar got a laugh, but not today. My comment was followed by a chorus of resentful swearing and disbelief from the rest. Every one of us had given up more lucrative opportunities to work in the bush, and treated each animal as something we had a great and personal responsibility for. The snares are incomparably destructive, trapping any animal that walks through, killing them through slow strangulation or gangrene as their limbs are garroted.

We desultorily ripped a few from the branches they were attached to, but knew this was too big a job for us on that day. At some point people from the village that bordered the reserve must have learned that no one in authority was able to patrol anywhere north of the river, and seen an opportunity. While I loathed the poachers, hated them for their cruelty and their methods, I knew that most were not doing this for commercial reasons. My rage was hypocritical, because I was perfectly aware that you rarely meet a starving conservationist.

Up to this point I had been feeling nothing but wild abandon interspersed with healthy dollops of fear during our adventure. The sense of boundless space, of eternal wilderness, was gone now, replaced by the sad knowledge that no matter the size of our reserve, we were isolated, with outside human needs encroaching and taking priority over those of the animals that I so adored. This reserve was a luxury, any wild space was a luxury, and as much fun as it was dicking around on a rubber raft, we guides had a greater responsibility. Our lives in the bush couldn't be just about fun.

With this realization came another one, just as sobering. Snares were a poor man's tool of choice when hunting, whether for meat or the incredibly valuable rhinoceros that we had in our area. But some poachers use guns. Africa is a continent where firearms are as cheap as the lives they take, and now every bush, every tree trunk seemed a potential hiding place, not just for a predator but for someone with malicious intent. I started scanning the bush more closely, hoping not to see the dull blue-gray of a rifle barrel pointing at us.

Our track hit a crossways, the path it met broader and more firmly packed. This was a hippo trail, their neat gait making two tight parallel lines, with a thin grassy strip in between, like a smaller version of the roads our Land Rovers used. This had to lead back to the river, as hippos needed to be back in the water each day. We grew less grim as we headed back, ready to resume our rafting, but now our mission had taken on some urgency. We wanted to be back as soon as possible to report what was happening north of the river, and use whatever means we had at our disposal to stop it.

The path was broad enough for us to trot, the low branches trapping humid air and making us pant wetly, until, huffing, we came to the water. The hippos started a chorus of snorting again, but they were upstream from us now, and we leaped onto *Lollipop* and set ourselves afloat, the current quickly picking us up, bouncing us over rocks, then splitting into narrower channels that we negotiated at leisure, enjoying the vibrant bird life and ignoring the occasional branch-entangled plastic bag that was a reminder of the world outside.

We floated over places that only weeks before I had walked upon, once-sandy beaches that were perfect spots for sundowner drinks now submerged, a haven for fish and other marine life.

"Croc?" Iain said, pointing at a spot perturbingly close to us. "I think I saw a croc," he repeated, this time with more conviction. This could end in seconds, a croc snagging one of us from off the side, or taking hold of a dangling leg from underwater. My toes developed a life of their own and curled, as if trying to retract turtle-like into my feet. The paddles beat the water again. I doubted the efficiency of this method to deter predators, and wondered if it might not even attract them.

"Not a big one, though," Iain added, information I would have dearly liked more promptly. "Only about six feet," he added, and my toes curled again, considering this more than large enough to do them harm. The rest of my extremities agreed, as did my limbs, and I had a very strong urge just to curl fetally around one of the other guy's heads until we were safe.

Instead I took one of the machetes and paddled with a little more vigor than was needed, again turning us into a spin and wrapping the dinghy around us.

"Sorry, sorry," I said, trying to reverse our direction with little success. People rarely believe me when I explain just how uncoordinated I am, and only take me seriously once they have seen my ineptitude in action. This was a prime example and left the others gobsmacked as I steered our raft at full speed directly into a menacing-looking accumulation of detritus in the middle of the river.

We were by now in deep water again, and only a few hundred meters from the causeway where Alpheus should be waiting for us. But we were stuck fast. *Lollipop* had hit side-on, her right-hand hull wedged firmly against a stump, the jolt tearing everyone except me out of the doughnut holes and flinging them into the river. This saved them, but doomed me. The lift generated on the now-empty side by the branch had a fulcrum effect on the hull where I sat. The small security the hole once offered now became a curse as my legs were crimped in, impossible to shake free, one ankle betraying me and finding a gap in the submerged branches to snake through, just as my upper torso and head were forced under the water.

I saw only the rippled surface of the river desperate inches from my nose and mouth, and heard water rush into my ears, find nothing of interest there, then depart to investigate places downstream.

Unlike Iain, Justin, and Duncan, I was not aerobically fit, and only knew what a gym looked like from being dragged once by Iain. But desperation gave my underdeveloped abdominals the strength to sit me up, just far enough that my nostrils just pierced the surface, then my lips. I gulped air greedily, but was dragged back under. A branch the river had carried this far hit the top of my head painfully, and again I bolted up, belched river water, and regretted the exhalation, as before I could draw much-needed oxygen to my lungs my midsection quivered against the irresistible rush of water, and I was drowning.

"Okay," a calm voice inside me said, amongst the panic. "This is okay."

Just one breath in was all I wanted, the small rational part of my brain yelling angrily at me not to do it, but the urge was too seductive, wheedling at me to just take a sip of air, even though there was none to be had, my lungs burning, the river water now looking red as blood vessels burst in my eyes, no sound now, then shock as I inhaled. Water went through my nostrils, polluted my sinuses, then splashed into my lungs which rejected it immediately, making me gag and draw more liquid in.

I've heard it said that drowning is peaceful, a beautiful way to die, but have never known who could possibly have reported that. This was not at all relaxing. My passivity disappeared. I wanted to thrash, to scream, to protest in some violent way, but had no strength available, no will left for it.

Busy as I was dying, I gave no thought to my friends, who due to my actions had been ejected to parts of the river unknown. Downstream from the island we had struck was nothing but open water, a happy hunting ground for larger crocodiles seeking any creature as inept at paddling as a human.

What I didn't know was that despite the violence of their ejection, all four had managed to grab onto the island before being swept away. Justin was the first to reach me, and rather than trying to hold me up, which would only have pushed him under, with incredible strength he simply wrenched the entire raft free. I felt a stronger surge as the fulcrum briefly intensified and I went deeper, then with my legs still in the doughnut hole I found myself popping skywards, surfacing with a splutter and leaking orifices. My eyes, ears, nose, and lungs ached, but I was alive, and while many people may not find being afloat on a tire tube in a raging river with crocodiles around them very pleasant, at that point I was absolutely delighted. I would have hugged Justin if he wasn't the sort of guy who'd punch your lights out for that. Instead I just thanked him weakly and did what I could to help the others back on board.

Alpheus was there as we paddled to the causeway, and watched as we inelegantly beached at its southern side, using the one oar we hadn't lost. He listened patiently as we told him of our day, smiling the same smile I'd seen him give to tourists on countless occasions, but never to his family or friends. Every now and then he'd say "Really?" and we'd assure him the adventures we were regaling him with were true. Other guides would later tell us that despite our mishaps along the way, they would have loved to come along. Alpheus, though, gave no indication that he'd wished he'd been with us.

Within six weeks the river had dropped enough for us to cross and start removing the snares, and begin to estimate how many of the animals that we knew had been killed. I stood in the place

where I had almost drowned, the island now just a sorry tangle
of dead branches and reeds pegged into dirty sand. Within the
same six weeks Alpheus's daughter died from an illness we all
guessed at but didn't want to name. I felt incredibly lucky to be
alive, and grateful for the opportunities afforded me, and that
I had the luxury of caring about little more than the lives of
animals.

A Kinky Tail

I fell in love with cheetahs at my very first sight of one, and it is an affair that has yet to end, but there was one who will always hold a special place for me.

Kinky Tail was born with a problem. She didn't have the usual long, flattened paddle of a tail that most cheetahs have; instead she bore a shortened appendage that was cocked half-way along its truncated length like a quizzical eyebrow. Yet she was a survivor, and from her litter of siblings she was the only one to make it to walking age.

We guides watched the lives of animals like it was an ongoing soap opera, knowing who was partnering with whom, who was gearing up for a hostile takeover, and wondering just who it was that had killed the other members of Kinky's litter. Unlike television, though, sometimes the most dramatic moments occurred off screen. We could only guess whether it was lions or hyenas that made Kinky an only child.

When I first saw her I was in the final stages of my training as a guide, looking for any and every excuse to go on the safari drives with other guides, but doubling my efforts if there were reports of Kinky and her mother in the area.

On one drive we watched her training to be a hunter. She wasn't using live bait, but rather the seed pod from a sausage tree. These pods are long, torpedo-shaped, and heavy, and have, in a breeze, rudely awoken many campers unwise enough to pitch their tents beneath them by spearing through the canvas. Kinky was unconcerned about danger from above, and intently batted her toy around, its irregular shape ensuring random

51

bounces that would thrill her so much she would give a bird-like twitter of excitement. Her mother didn't watch Kinky, but the area around her, making sure that nothing would take her last youngster away. On occasion the mother's tail would flick at a fly, its length almost the same as her lithe body, highlighting the difference between her perfect form and her daughter's abbreviated one. Kinky seemed unaware of any difference, though, and happily played with her sausage, delighting the tourists who sat only feet away in the vehicle, and deepening my feelings for her. I knew that many cheetahs never made it to adulthood, but had a feeling that Kinky would.

Her odds slimmed with a report that one of the guides training me brought in one day. Kinky Tail and her mother had been seen at the western edge of our reserve, which in itself was the western extremity of the Kruger National Park, a protected area of seven-and-a-half thousand square miles, larger than Israel or Ireland. Kinky's mother had been enticed to leave; likely she had spotted easy prey on the other side of the fence in the form of villager's goats. Making a mockery of the expensive, three-strand electrified eight-foot fence, she climbed a termite mound and hopped over. The goats had seen her climb and wisely scampered off. Kinky's mother followed the way they had gone, leaving her cub to wait, not knowing she couldn't make it back into the reserve, not knowing she was leaving its protection.

Reports came that Kinky's mother was killed by the villagers, in retaliation for what she did to their livestock. At the news I grew drunk on anger, and hated them for what they had done, refusing to think of how many people might have derived sustenance from that goat, and how easy it is to turn on beauty when it takes food from your table.

Kinky was still only ten months old, too young to be

independent. Male cheetahs take no part in rearing young, and to survive Kinky would have to learn how to catch items far more agile than sausage pods.

After affording us two more sightings, and looking increasingly thin, she disappeared, and the guides in the area resignedly agreed that she must have starved to death.

A few weeks later I was leading one of my first drives as a fully fledged guide. I heard the unmistakable snorting of impalas, and Titus pointed excitedly at a small herd of them making breakneck speed for a group of trees. Behind them came Kinky Tail, a glorious flash of yellow and black, her powerful stride keeping her airborne more often than on the ground.

She missed. The impala she had homed in on gave a desperate side step before leaping over some bushes, and Kinky overshot her mark, drawing to a stop in a cloud of dust.

The problem might have been her deformity. Cheetahs use their tails like rudders as they run, helping them steer at the ridiculous velocities that they can achieve. But Kinky only had her claws to dig in with, claws which remained unsheathed at all times like a sprinter's spikes, but in this instance they hadn't given enough traction for her to catch a meal.

The tourists I was leading must have become concerned about my emotional stability. I quivered with joy, even though she had been unsuccessful in her hunt. She didn't appear underfed, and I immediately formulated a theory that she must have started catching small prey, from lizards and ground dwelling birds up to the common-as-mud scrub hare, and was now moving up to the sort of meal that could keep her fed for days. If only she could catch it.

She panted deeply as we watched, drawing in oxygen to break down the lactic acid that builds after a cheetah's sprint. The tear lines on a cheetah's face give them a permanently mournful air, but there was an increased look of disconsolation every time she glanced the way the impalas had run, like a child denied an ice cream.

Finally she stood up, and ambled into some deep shade to recuperate. She wouldn't hunt again soon, being exhausted, so we left her there because the tourists were easily bored by an inactive animal.

We saw Kinky regularly after that, as she established a home range almost exactly the same as the one her mother had held. She became adept at hunting impala, judging their step and actually slowing herself down in preparation, ready to trip them when they were within range. She wasn't old enough to mate yet, but all the guides looked forward to the day when she had cubs of her own, as we couldn't imagine a cheetah that would make a better teacher.

In a life of setbacks, Kinky Tail took another blow. One day while chasing a small antelope called a steenbok, she didn't swerve out of the way of a burrow in the ground, and her leg disappeared into it and jammed while she was moving at a speed three times faster than an Olympic sprinter. She came to an abrupt halt, pivoting at an awkward angle before hauling her leg out. The guide who watched it all said she could barely limp into some thick woodland afterwards for shelter. She wasn't there that afternoon, and again we feared the worst. While cheetahs have the monopoly on speed in the animal kingdom, they aren't fighters, and Kinky wouldn't stand a chance against a leopard, lion, or hyena even when healthy. Disabled, she would be finished in no time.

As time passed, Kinky became just a sad footnote in the ongoing drama of the animals we watched. Bombi the leopard saw off a rival male, the dominant lions came together into their coalition of six for the first time in years, One Horn the rhino was seen mating, elephants were coming back into the area in numbers for the first time in months, and life and death went on without irritating commercials. Someone found a dead impala by a thicket, and called it in on the radio in case anyone was interested.

Iain went to check it out, as he was the sort of guide who liked carcasses—not for any morbid reasons, but because they could tell a story that he had the skills to interpret. This impala had been killed near the river, probably while coming down for a drink. The bush was thick, perfect habitat for a leopard. But the throat showed only the slightest marks of violence, as if something daintier had killed it. It was a typical cheetah kill, but the habitat was all wrong. Cheetahs need open areas where their speed is of the utmost advantage.

One of the trackers found the spoor of a cheetah nearby. There was a clear imperfection in the tracks, though, as one leg dragged badly. We knew it was Kinky. Cheetahs are not normally credited with the greatest intelligence, yet she'd taught herself to hunt as an ambush predator, lurking in bushes and nabbing prey as it passed by. She may never beat anyone at chess, but she was certainly smarter than your average cat.

We continued to find well-chewed antelope in odd places, but rarely saw Kinky anymore because her habitat was so dense, the sort of place you couldn't get even a Land Rover into. Going in on foot would be suicidal, not because cheetahs are at all dangerous to humans but because these riverside thickets were also where the few Cape buffalo in the reserve were likely to lurk, and a prime spot to startle the occasional hippo that was spending the day slumming on land. They wouldn't hesitate to stomp a guide to death.

I carried on with my first drives, wishing I was good enough to track Kinky Tail in the brush myself. A more experienced guide assured me I would be "a noted idiot" were I to try it.

Since idiocy is something I have rarely shied away from, I did go looking for her, and as testimony to my tracking skills at the time found nothing. No buffalo charged me, no hippo thundered from the reeds to snap me in half, and every time I was sure that the tracks I was looking at were those of a cheetah I would see hand prints in front of them and be forced to concede that it was baboons that had passed that way.

Another guide did find Kinky Tail, though, only a few weeks later.

She was dying. Abscesses had formed on each hip, she was emaciated and listless. He stood guard while a collection of guides and camp managers decided what to do. There was a strict if heartbreaking policy of noninterference in the lives of the animals that we watched, knew, and loved. But a loophole existed. Endangered species could be given assistance, particularly if their ailment was at the hand of man. Since all of Kinky's struggles began when her mother was killed, we warped the rules to suit her and called in a vet from the Kruger Park.

He arrived in an official-looking khaki vehicle, a mustachioed man with an air of quiet competence. With little preamble he loaded a pink-tufted dart into an air rifle, took aim from his vehicle some distance from Kinky ("If she lives, you don't want her running from your cars, thinking she'll get a sting in her backside," he later explained), and expertly hit her in her bony rump.

She took off. Even with only three functioning legs, her speed was still a sight to behold as she raced through mercifully open ground, before faltering, giving a confused chirp, and collapsing more than two hundred yards from where she'd taken the dart. It had taken her only seconds to cover the ground.

We approached in the vehicles, and found her panting, twitching, like a dog chasing rabbits in its sleep. Up close she looked fragile, paper thin, and only a sip of air away from death. The vet quickly rubbed a lotion onto her eyes to stop them from drying out while she was paralyzed, and injected a sedative, explaining as he did that the dart had made her incapable of movement, but that she was still fully conscious. "We need to handle her, and the sedative will make it less stressful for her, but it isn't strong because I don't think she could take it."

With a deft manual examination he announced that she had dislocated a hip, and to avoid the pain of lying on it she had always rested on her other side, creating an abscess. Then she had swapped sides, making a wound there too. She had somehow stayed alive like this for weeks, he said, judging by the advanced state of the injuries. "Helluva tough cheetah," he said respectfully.

When it came time to load her into the veterinary van, I was honored that the others suggested I pick her up. New to the bush, I didn't feel I deserved such close handling but took the opportunity with a mixture of delight and sadness. I knew that a female cheetah should weigh around seventy-five pounds, but Kinky was light like a child, her form draping over my arms. I luxuriated in the sensation of holding a big cat, a *wild* big cat in my arms, but only for a moment. A deep bone-trembling rumble came from Kinky Tail. Her growl vibrated through my sternum and drove the air from my lungs, and I'm convinced it pushed through me so hard it made hair grow on my back. Now it was I that felt fragile, and when the vet said, "Maybe you should load her in," I quickly but gently obliged.

He drove off, promising to call, and I felt like a concerned parent, desperately hoping this man would phone.

He did call, and he had good news. Kinky had grown a lump on the hip that had acted as a false socket for her dislocated limb, which he had filed down once he had relocated the leg. For her recovery to be successful she would need to be isolated from other animals for weeks, in a specially built enclosure, called a *boma*, fed by people who walked—not drove—to her enclosure and threw the meat over a screen so she wouldn't learn to associate the sound of vehicles or the sight of humans as being providers. "The problem," he said, "is that we don't have that sort of enclosure here, and don't have the funds to build it. She came from private land, so your lodge owners will have to pay for it to be done there."

Not a problem, we confidently assured him, and agreed that we would have a boma, made out of reeds and branches, built by the time her two-week recovery from surgery was up.

It was a problem. Not one of the land owners in the area thought it was a worthwhile cause. Apparently the cheetah that was an unwitting movie star in the videos of so many tourists, that had provided joy and education for a global audience, was not worth saving.

Finally Duncan, Iain, Devlin, Justin, and I convinced the owner of the camp where we worked to let us build the *boma* on his property—but at our own expense. As the only non–South

African employee, I wasn't used to thinking in rands, and knew only that my pay amounted to $125 a month. The others made more, but none of us were loaded down with weighty bank balances.

Yet there was no question of what we would do. With a commitment of time and money from other guides in the region, we started communicating with the outside world to see if someone could sell us cheap building materials. I was no good with a hammer, so knew I would feel useless when building started, and spoke no Afrikaans, the language of most store owners in the area, so felt all I could do was give my money. I gave it all, thinking I had never spent a better dollar.

On the day that a truck we had arranged to pick up the goods was set to depart, Iain phoned the vet to ask how Kinky Tail was doing.

There was a pause on the other end of the line.

"You mean you haven't been told?"

Iain felt dread, but asked anyway, "Didn't she make it?"

"Oh no, she was fine after the surgery. Quite a tough bird. Word got around about what you guys were up to with the *boma*, and I got a call from Mick Muslight." This was the name of the man who oversaw the entire group of private and commercial lodges in the region, as well as owning one of the larger operations himself.

I'd been disappointed to learn that this bush outpost was as political as anywhere else that had more than two people, and had heard whispers of nefarious goings-on, plots to make the east of the reserve more successful than the west, ideas that seemed quite silly until now. "He said that your cheetah was poor genetic stock, and wouldn't be allowed back in. I had to put her down." And with an apology, the conversation ended.

Iain raged, and hit a timber pole hard enough to shake the building.

I was just as apoplectic. "Poor genetic stock? Poor genetic stock!?" I frothed, "She was the best animal out there!" I stopped talking, thinking furiously that bald men with high cholesterol shouldn't be allowed to judge anything's DNA, but was afraid that I would cry if I tried to say so.

The reserve had felt boundless and wild to me only moments before, and now it changed. Man loomed large over it, and I felt that I hadn't escaped the outside world as thoroughly as I had imagined. Powerlines encroached, dams were unnatural, and the priapic telephone tower was an easy joke waiting to be made about man's need to conquer everything.

There and then I decided that I would leave here, and find a wilder place. I'd find somewhere that Kinky Tail wouldn't have died from a needle, and where human politics had no part. I'd heard whisperings about a place to the north, a place that people said was the real bush.

I would go to Botswana.

THE GIGGLER

Lions have charged me, buffalo too. Elephants have pursued me with a fury and menace terrifying in any creature, let alone one as large as they are. Cobras and mambas have reared at me, their fangs glistening with venom, and of course just the presence of a crocodile makes my bowels squirm and consider evacuating.

But the most terrifying wildlife encounter I have ever had was not in a game reserve, nor from an animal with four legs. It was off the east coast of South Africa, somewhere north of the seaside town of Durban.

I have a habit of taking up hobbies for which some of my unusual physical traits leave me poorly equipped. Skiing is one. Every few years I try it, only to discover that I still do not possess the right kind of pelvis. No matter how patient (or how angry) my instructor, my legs drift apart until I am in danger of tearing myself asunder, and with a yelp I throw myself sideways, knowing that a searing faceful of snow is better than a prolapsed rectum. Birdwatching, while something I still pursue, is another challenge, as I find it near impossible to locate a bird by call. Instead I am left wandering randomly, as my ears and brain don't communicate properly and I hear sounds coming from the opposite direction of their real emission.

Of all my pursuits, though, scuba diving was undoubtedly the one activity I should have done my utmost to avoid, due to two inborn impairments. The first is that despite being of average physical size in all other respects, my lungs are enormous. No matter what Zen-like calm I attempt, as I go into an alien environment I become excited and inhale mightily, so in a few short moments I can drain even the largest scuba tanks. This forces my ascent to wait bobbing next to the boat for the other divers to complete their excursion.

Which is where the second impediment comes into play. With just the slightest ripple I am overwhelmed by nausea, turn a pasty khaki, and offer anything to the boat skipper to abandon those below and head for shore, pronto. I would do anything not to be motion sick, for the obvious reason of it being unspeakably awful, but also because the nausea hovers and cripples me all day. I have offered many tokens as bribes for a shore return: money, free safaris, my sister, and anything else I can think of to be taken back, but have always been denied by the professionalism of the skippers.

After Kinky Tail's death I had felt the need to get away from the bush altogether, and spend some time in as different an environment as possible. I'd signed up for a shark course, popped some motion-sickness pills, and found myself on my way to a dive site.

This particular dive had started poorly for me. We had done the obligatory and indisputably valuable equipment check before taking gear to the boat. Once aboard we checked everything again, which is safe and sane as scuba diving puts you in an element not your own, and safety should be a paramount concern. Then, after forty or so minutes of pounding over the ocean while I controlled my breathing and watched the horizon intently, our group of ten checked their gear one last time, which to me was just overkill, unnecessary, cruel, mean, nasty, and I quietly pleaded for everyone to hurry up. I rarely felt sick on the outward ride, but in the few minutes that we sat bobbing, dipping, and rising over the site, the smell of boat fuel invading my nostrils and the up and down, up and down of the boat set me to retching as I fumbled for flipper straps and tightened my mask.

We had spent almost a week in class, learning from an expert about shark identification, shark biology, shark behavior, and had even dissected a shark caught by local fisherman and learned that it was pregnant, a sad tragedy for this dwindling family of fish. Now, though, after chomping at the bit the whole time, our entry into the water to interact with the real thing was delayed. By Germans.

This couple had sat through the course with stoic intensity, absorbing the fascinating information with no visible pleasure, only showing emotion when they registered contempt for the class clown, which was me, and his jokes. Their obvious disdain didn't particularly bother me, as I found it hard to respect people who took themselves so seriously yet had grown incongruously flippant dreadlocks. The dark, lank strands of their hair contrasted with their pale and unhealthy complexions, as if deceased rodents were hanging from their scalp.

Now the German man was sweeping chunks of hair from his face, and assisting his girlfriend as she showed an incredible lack of dexterity in putting together the octopus-like arrangements of tubes and cords that make up a scuba rig. I knew I was turning green, because the person beside me, a South African, said, "Yerra man, you look like you're about to kotch."

I didn't answer. Instead I alternated staring at the wavering horizon, and glaring at the Germans, who were Teutonically and methodically double-checking that which had already been triple-checked. "Oh come on!" I wanted to scream, but I have never been confrontational enough for my own good, and feared that opening my mouth would lead to something more unpleasant for everyone than words. I would have just jumped in the water and waited there, but one of the golden rules of diving in this size group is that you have to all enter at the same time, form a "hot tub" a few meters from the boat, and descend as a group.

The Germans were finally rigged, and I took some reassurance from seeing that a few of my fellow classmates were looking pale and shooting impatient glances at them. The dreadlocked man did the last test of his system, quickly turning the air on and off again to make sure it flowed. Turning awkwardly on the inflatable's side, his wetsuit squeaking against the canvas, he did the same to his girlfriend's rig, yanking the dial on, only for it to give a viciously loud pop. A small fragment of rubber whipped the length of boat before disappearing to sea. Compressed air gushed and whistled from the tank, as the German girl pulled a series of stricken facial expressions. Her boyfriend sat hulking and useless while the instructor scrambled to their end of the boat and turned her air off.

"We need to get her a new tank," he said, "so you'll have to rig up again."

I don't know what they said to that, because with a defiant thought of "Bugger that," I had splashed over the side. More bodies followed, and the little rebellion I had started soon included all of my classmates except the Germans. The instructor told us we were idiots, because the whole reason we were at this very spot was for its unusually high density of sharks. One thing we had learned is that a diver is most likely to be attacked while on the surface. But being in the water was relief from the seasickness, a force so powerful that being bitten in two seemed pleasant by comparison.

While their preparations had seemed to take an eon previously, now that I was bobbing comfortably away they seemed much faster, and soon we were towed to the actual dive site, a place known as The Cathedral. Down we went, all busy checking the gauges that measured the rate of descent, the amount of air in our tanks, the time of the dive, and deflating our buoyancy compensator vests, kicking for extra propulsion, while adjusting our masks better to see the beautiful arena that awaited us.

There was an underwater plain, edged by a dramatic sheer cliff that dropped away to impenetrable depths. There was a crater in the plain, as if some cataclysmic space object had once smashed into it, and in this depression swam sharks, in numbers too breathtaking to attempt counting. It should have been frightening, even though we knew that these were harmless raggy-tooth sharks (known to me from Australian waters as gray nurses, and to the Americans in the group as sand tigers), but the docility of their lazy turns within The Cathedral was calming, mesmerizing, and seductive enough that I wanted to join them.

All seasickness was forgotten, any residual frustration with the Germans long gone, and I felt the peace that comes underwater, felt a passion for these sharks, ugly in photos but with a grace in movement that would shame any dancer. With these emotions high, the next physical trait that should have precluded me from diving kicked in. I gave a small snort, the sort of sound that in the burble and gurgle in the underwater cacophony will go unnoticed, but this was quickly followed by a gleeful high-pitched laugh. This pierced through the Darth Vader—ish breathing sounds of the group, the occasional clank of a spare regulator against a tank, and the harsh rasp of Velcro as someone opened a pocket. The silly sound that I had made amused me more than it should, so I let out a longer series of barely restrained happy squirrel noises, and I knew that I was drunk again, but didn't care.

In diving there is something known as Martini's Law: The nitrogen in the mix you breathe has a narcotic effect that becomes more pronounced with depth, and each ten meters down you go is allegedly equivalent to one cocktail. From previous experience I knew that biology poured me stiff drinks, because at only ten meters everything seemed far more amusing than it really should be, and I started a sort of squeaky laughter around my mouthpiece. Sound, I had learned, traveled faster underwater, so in no time my sonic bullets of amusement would start irritating the crap out of my fellow divers, who were just trying to enjoy the peace of the underwater world. Pushing thirty meters as we were now, I was miles from sobriety, and while I didn't wish to be annoying, I could not stifle my glee.

I finned my way over the lip of the ledge to a place that the dive master had told us about. The crater from above was beautiful, but this vantage point was truly breathtaking because it opened straight into the circling sharks. A natural archway had formed in the cliff face, giving a window directly into the swirl of sharks, and taking a handhold I chortled away as an eight-foot shark swam within inches of my nose. From its pale goat's eye it was impossible to see what it thought of my mania, but even with a mask on and the occasional grease-trailing dreadlock obscuring him I could see that the German, as ever, was not amused by me. The look he gave me suggested I was some dastardly villain from a Batman comic. "I am The Giggler," I thought, then imagined myself on a crime spree, dressed only in a wetsuit, wearing my underpants on the outside. This sent me into paroxysms of laughter, so when a small swell washed me forward I lost my grip and bumped straight into one of the sharks.

A flash of lucidity pierced my narcosis. No matter how docile these creatures might ordinarily be, they were still sharks, and head-butting them was without a doubt no laughing matter. Yet a small "tee-hee" slipped out and I was away again, looking for the exact shark that I had offended so I could give it the international diving signal for "I'm sorry."

But I couldn't see it, or any other sharks for that matter. They had all vanished. Snorting air from my nose and fogging my mask, I turned with an elegance that I could never achieve on land and looked around for them. Nothing. No sharks, no fish, no movement, except my fellow divers, still slowly finning, checking their gauges, doing the myriad small things divers do.

I maintained my slow pirouette, enjoying the comical burble of my exhalations and wondering without any great concern where all the raggies had gone. I was the last in the line of ten divers who were now strung out at the edge of the plateau, and I noticed as I looked down the group's parade formation how motionless everyone had become. Like attentive meerkats they were all facing the same direction, and looking into the gloomy gray of the ocean, I saw a shape coming at us.

I stopped giggling. I held my breath. I watched as it easily covered the distance to us and with only the barest movement, terrifyingly casual, swam along our line. I had always wanted to see a great white shark, but suddenly couldn't recall a single good reason why. Never in my life, even with crocodiles, have I seen an animal that looked more like its entire purpose on Earth was to eat me. My heart ratcheted to a pace that may have permanently damaged my ribs, and a lump formed in my throat as if I was going to cry. Even while doing so little, the shark exhibited a callous power, a raw ability to inspire terror that I had never conceived.

The shark cruised past each of us, like a malevolent general inspecting his troops, and I did my utmost not to draw attention to myself. With my joints locked and extremities curled I did what I could to appear like driftwood, and saw that my fellow divers were doing the same. Ten of us sank slowly, only a gauge here, a stray dreadlock there flapping, everything else still.

"It's not looking at me," I thought to myself. "Please let it not be looking at me," I pleaded to Neptune, Poseidon, or whoever would listen. There was no aggression in the shark's movement, just a palpable menace in its form, a blood-freezing capability to sever body parts and drain a person of liquids. My limbs wanted to jerk and flail, but with a sober focus unimaginable moments before, they held their rigidity. As the shark reached the end of the line and drew level with me I stared directly into its black, soulless eye.

A sliver of white appeared at the edge of its pupil as it passed, indicating that the orb had swiveled on its stalk.

"Oh bugger, it's looking at me."

But with languid sweeps of its giant tail it carried on, into the gloom of the ocean, which was now the most oppressive environment I had ever been in. My lungs ached, and I realized that I had held my breath throughout the encounter, and with one gulp I sucked my tank close to dry.

I dared to shift, and with a movement that I hoped mimicked something not very tasty I turned, and watched the great white lazily fin its way into invisibility, somewhere only twenty yards away. I wanted out. The eyes of my fellow divers were wide, some in terror, some twinkling with wonder, a few with a crazed delight that I could not share. My air gauge read close to empty, and I signaled to the dive master my intent to ascend. He checked the rest of the group, who to my bewilderment were content to stay longer, so I went up alone.

Never go faster than your slowest bubble, is the rule. Don't hold your breath, or it will expand in your lungs and burst them, is another. The urge, though, was to sprint, finning madly and launching like a porpoise into the boat. Fortunately some sobriety returned with diminished depth, and I maintained a sedate pace. One of my favorite aspects of the underwater domain had always been the widening of the world, the unique perspective of having a view above, around, and below all at once, but now this experience was filled with a looming menace.

I broke the surface and searched for the boat. The skipper was following a float attached by a long cord to the dive master, and the current had drawn me away from them. I whistled for the boat, but he couldn't hear me over the putter of his engine and the sound of the waves. I inflated my vest for maximum buoyancy, and struck out with a swimming stroke that I knew was too graceless to be mistaken for a seal's motion, yet hoped was more impressive than that of an appealingly injured fish.

I flipped to backstroke for a view behind me, expecting a looming fin, desperately trying to drive out the famous *"Da-Dum! Da-Dum"* music that was lodged in my brain. I was ready for a flurry if such a fin did appear, but also knew my efforts would be ridiculous, as even the quickest humans in the water are barely faster than kelp.

Finally the skipper heard my whistles, and brought the inflatable to me at a speed that seemed cruelly ponderous. I already had my weight belt in hand as he drew alongside, and flung it with vigor into the boat where it clanged against something metallic.

I gave the most almighty kick of my fins and hauled myself into the vessel, the first time I had ever managed the feat without the indignity of someone hauling on my vest from behind.

"Shark," I spluttered to the skipper, who beamed back at me.

"Great, man," he said.

"Great white," I replied.

"What?"

"White!" I insisted.

"Wow!"

"Yeah."

I sat huffing, stripping off the heavy paraphernalia that had allowed me to breathe underwater.

"Hmph," the skipper said appreciatively. "Nice," he added, clearly not sharing my view that a torpedo with teeth was impressive, worthy of respect, but not "nice." He looked at me, I was still breathing heavily, not from exertion anymore, but the long, concentrated huffs of a man trying to focus on anything but the nausea that was gathering like greasy storm clouds.

"Hey man, you going to puke? Maybe you should get over the side. . . . "

On other dives I'd done before this course, I'd found that immersion reduced my motion sickness, so clung to the side of the inflatable while I waited for my teeny-lunged companions to emerge. Sharks had only ever briefly entered my mind on those occasions, and when they did I'd draw my legs to the underside of the vessel, hugging them in to reduce their dangly profile. After seeing the white I didn't want to even contemplate dipping a toe into the water again, at least for a day or so, and tried to suggest this with a look to the skipper, but he was busy tracking the float again. The forward motion alleviated my concerns somewhat, but the waft on the air of blue exhaust countered it, and I started feeling hot and prickly in my wetsuit.

As I was living the life of a budget traveler, and owned nothing that wouldn't fit into my backpack, the wetsuit was not mine. It was a rental, and like every rental wetsuit in the world had been sorely abused by the people who had hired it. I know of no other common courtesy in the world as frequently ignored as the one that declares that you should not pee in a wetsuit that someone will use after you. When I unzipped and peeled the wetsuit away from my flesh, the acrid tang of a thousand urinations overcame me, and I was violently ill.

The attack was so sudden that I hadn't turned my head fully in time, and some landed in the boat.

"Excuse me," I gasped, and aimed my next effluxion with more consideration. I overcame some fear and reached into the water to splash onto my face, and making a scoop liberally watered down the mess in the boat, noting with some satisfaction that the only equipment it had hit had a name tag on it that read "Gunther."

After what seemed an eternity, the other divers started popping to the surface, one or two noting what a fine collection of fish they had seen feeding immediately around the boat, but most still babbling excitingly about the great white. All talk was muted as soon as we set off for shore, pounding over waves and turning our wind-whipped and tear-streaming faces into the salt spray.

On shore we all started talking again, and I recovered enough to join in. "Fantastic!" I finally said, it suddenly dawning on me that this was an experience people paid hundreds of dollars for, to do in the artificial circumstance of a cage with a shark baited by pouring blood into the water.

I realized something else as well. I wasn't afraid to go back in the water. I must have swum with sharks hundreds of times without even knowing they were there, and just like the one today they had done nothing but show some curiosity which had turned into indifference.

I could live with indifference from a shark, but wanted peace with my fellow species, so as the group sat on the beach that night I approached Gunther and his girlfriend, made some comments about how great the dive had been, and in the spirit of reconciliation said, "So, do you want to go for a swim?"

"Chew are crazy Aussie!" he answered, his accent thick, then added, "but okay."

We dived in, his girlfriend followed, and one by one the rest of the group joined us. We splashed around, even those who earlier had said they might never swim again. Then someone shouted "Shark!" and all we did was laugh.

WELCOME TO BOTSWANA

"Hi, you must be Peter?" said the man as he locked the office door and stepped into the dusty courtyard. The mangiest-looking cat I'd ever seen slunk away from him, and hissed at us both.

"Yes," I said, my mouth too dry to say more. I had just driven from Johannesburg to Maun, across the Kalahari Desert in the December heat behind the wheel of an open safari vehicle. It had been a hellacious trip. I was sunburnt. Tired. Bruised. At one point, as I crossed open country, a single cloud appeared and unleashed a torrent of rain over my roofless vehicle. This was one of the many indignities I had suffered on the drive.

To see the road during the rainstorm, I had turned on the wipers. One of these had given one swipe on the modified windscreen, not liked the odd angle, dislodged from its mount, flipped over the screen, and hit me in the forehead. As well as my dented head, I was chafed from sitting on the wet foam of the seat, and my entire aroma was somewhat goatish.

My mood was as damp as my pants, but lifted periodically with the thought, "I'm in Botswana!" This was followed by, "To be a safari guide!" And even though I'd been a guide for a year already in South Africa, this seemed so exotic that my burnt face would peel into painful creases as I smiled.

But the man greeting me seemed determined to drag me back down. My belief was that all I had to do was to get to Maun, and I'd have a job. Instead I was told that if I had been only an hour earlier I could have gone to the motor registry before it shut for Christmas (it was the 24th), had Botswana number plates put on the vehicle, and carried on driving to the camp where I would be at least temporarily based.

"Duba! The most remote camp in Botswana!" the man, who had now introduced himself as Alan, bragged. "But now you'll have to wait until the 27th when the registry reopens, get the vehicle legit, then off you go."

He gave me directions through the town (not hard; it has one turning circle and no traffic lights) to a house the company owned, a key for the door, and instructions to meet him back there in three days' time.

The next day was Christmas; the day after, my birthday. The few stores in town were shut, and while out of politeness I initially resisted eating the Christmas mince pies in the refrigerator, I ended up having them for Christmas lunch, and dinner. Having broken the seal of morality, I then drank the beer in the fridge as well. On my twenty-second birthday I ate the last pies, and drank the last beer. I got a bellyache. And right behind the point on my forehead that was already peeling, I got a headache too. "Welcome to Botswana," I thought, and let a wash of self-pity and loneliness overcome me.

When I'd left my job in South Africa, not knowing where I was going next or if anyone would consider hiring me, I had been knotted by nerves, and felt my first twinge of adult stress. I missed the animals I had come to know, and still mourned Kinky Tail. I had some experience now, but wasn't sure how good I was at the job. My knowledge levels were mediocre, and my driving had been charitably described as adventurous—which only meant that I might occasionally have been trying to go over things when I ran into them. I did have one saving grace. No matter how many times I have seen elephants, antelopes, or ostriches, I'll still bounce around in excitement, an enthusiasm that transmits like an infection to the tourists who accompanied me.

"I get twitchy around animals" is not a line that works on a résumé, though, so I never used it. In fact, I never used a résumé at all. The interview process, I thought, was remarkably simple.

"You'd like a job? Sure. We need a guide in Botswana," the personnel manager had said. Wow, I'd thought, that was easy! Then came the catch, "Can you drive a vehicle up there for us?"

"No worries!" I'd assured my new boss, and hadn't had any, not thinking of the stress of driving a clearly commercial vehicle through a border post while asking for a tourist visa, not thinking that no hat will stay on your head at sixty miles per hour when you don't have a roof and that the sun block I'd applied would act like flypaper, trapping every bug, including small wasps, before melting stingingly into my eyes. I was completely unaware that after I had the vehicle registered, my journey would only have just begun.

The office was open again on the 27th, and far more lively than on Christmas Eve, a bustle of activity with men swarming on my vehicle as soon as it arrived, loading cooking oil, tinned goods, a drum of paraffin, and boxes of screws and nails for building works. These were all things too heavy to put in the light aircraft that the company used as aerial ferries, and they didn't seem to be doing the vehicle much good either. Its suspension groaned, and the back sat ominously low, lifting the front high and making me wonder if I'd have enough purchase to steer.

"Okay, Peter, are you ready?"

No, I thought, but instead asked, "Um, how do I get there?"

Alan smiled, a flash of gold in his teeth. "Dorcas will help you. She knows the way to Duba, don't you?"

He was addressing a large African woman who would take up both seats still available on the precariously laden vehicle. In reply to Alan she just tilted her head sideways, which did not seem like a definitive "Oh yes, Alan, like the back of my hand!" to me.

In moments we were off, and I soon exhausted my three words of Setswana, Dorcas her limited English, and the tar its resistance to potholes. We jolted along until the bedraggled road turned mercifully to dirt. We were heading northwest, around the world's largest oasis, on a journey of unknown length. When I'd asked for an expected duration everyone had just shrugged, something I would learn is common in Botswana—who knows if you will get lost, how many punctures you'll have, whether you will get repeatedly stuck in wet mud or dry soft sand, so nobody hazards an answer. Once at the camp, Alan said I would start guiding, something I was desperate to begin in this exotic and wild place.

There were few signposts, only the occasional warning that the road was about to pass through a village. These had surprisingly unimaginative names for Africa—Betsa, Eretsa, and the Etsas—starting at Etsa 6, then jumping to Etsa 12 for no reason that I could tell. When I asked Dorcas what the names meant, she just tilted her head at me as if it was a stupid question.

In these villages donkeys stood listlessly by the roads, some with their front legs tied together so they couldn't stray far. This seemed cruel to me, particularly because from what I could see nobody used the donkeys for anything except to occasionally pull a cobbled-together cart.

The air was rank with the smell of wild sage, and every time the light breeze shifted our dust trail would overtake us, coating us in fine Kalahari sand. Despite this, I was grinning. To our right as we drove I could see banks of reeds and papyrus. I was about to plunge headlong into the Okavango Delta, and couldn't be happier.

More donkeys on the road announced that we were approaching another village, and it was time for us to leave the road we were on. This was Shakawe, a village at the very point that the Delta went from being a normal waterway to a sprawling oasis. The Okavango River that fed it was the largest in the world not to reach an ocean. Instead, fault lines blocked its path and steered it into the Kalahari. At Shakawe the river dropped between two parallel faults before spreading out in the shape of a hand into the desert. We needed to get to the northeastern side of the Delta, and the purpose of our long drive so far had been to bring us here, a crossing for vehicles. After paying our fare I cautiously drove the vehicle onto a barge that felt barely large enough for its load. Two shirtless men, their black backs knotted with muscles, started cranking, and a cable rose from the water, thrumming in time with their exertions.

The boat wobbled, and I knew that there might be crocs around, but for once didn't particularly care. The air was alive with life, from midges and dragonflies to the birds that chased them, shouts from each shore, and the smell of the tannin-rich water. I saw two species I'd never seen before, which as a burgeoning birdwatcher made me brim with bonhomie.

As soon as we were off the ferry and hit the sandy bank, some nervous flutters began in my entrails. Vehicle tracks went every which way. Some straight, some left, some looping. Some, apparently drunk, went right back into the river.

"Dorcas?" I indicated the swirl, and fulfilling my premonition she just cocked her head. "That doesn't help," I added, my mood fading. "You do know the way, don't you?" I had a sudden image of myself living in Shakawe forever, slowly selling off auto parts to survive.

Dorcas ignored me, and instead whistled to a young man in tattered shorts, then shouted at him in a long stream of Setswana. He strolled over, a pace so leisurely it suggested he was the only young man in the world who actually believed speed could kill you.

"*Yebo* mama," he said to her, and nodded casually to me as if we were old acquaintances and no introduction was needed, then hauled himself into the same row of seats as Dorcas. He seemed unfazed by the lack of seat space beside his hefty traveling companion. I watched fascinated as he squeezed onto the seat beside her, like a hard-boiled egg getting into a bottle.

"He knows the way," Dorcas said, the longest sentence we had shared.

"Hi! I'm Peter!" I said in as friendly a voice as I could, wanting him to like me and know that I wasn't one of those white guys who would just ignore him. Instead, he ignored me, except to point a finger at one of the many tracks.

We drove it for more than an hour, through thorny acacia landscape, not hugging the edge of the Delta like I thought we would. Instead, after more than an hour we arrived at a village that by the standards of the other side of the river seemed poorer, their donkeys thinner, the children less enthusiastic when chasing the car and asking for sweets.

"Stop! Stop here!" the young man commanded me. I ground to a halt, the brakes rasping at the fine sand that was forming a paste on the discs.

He called into a hut, and an older man appeared, dressed in a shirt and trousers.

"My uncle," the young man said, finally gracing me with a smile, "he knows the way."

Oh bugger, I thought, I see where this is heading, and the "uncle" (a term used very loosely in Africa) climbed the vehicle's frame. Once aboard, the young man hopped out, gave us a cheery wave, and ambled off to talk to some pretty girls who had been watching us with disinterested, heavy-lidded eyes.

"*Dumela Rra,*" Uncle said, greeting me in Setswana. I returned the greeting, at which point he decided I must be fluent and rattled off a stream of words as unstoppable as a rhino. Trying something, I cocked my head to the side. He laughed, and with a universal gesture indicated for me to carry on ahead.

To the next village. Where he departed. But his brother knew the way.

And so it went. I knew that I was now a modern version of the village idiot, an eternal taxi man until fuel ran out, at which point I would probably have tomatoes thrown at me, or whatever these people did for cheap entertainment.

After what seemed like half a day, one made a mistake. We found the camp.

I was quite shocked, delighted, relieved, and even more sunburnt, all of which made me a little giddy.

We drove into the back of the camp and I pulled up beside a dilapidated old Toyota. Dorcas said, "Thanks, *Rra,*" and with remarkable agility for her size hopped from the vehicle, grabbed the many nylon bags she had brought, and scurried away.

I stood there, not knowing what to do next, feeling very out of place.

"Hey," a sharp voice commanded. "You're late!" I'd had no idea I was on a schedule, and really didn't want to explain that I'd been so easily taken advantage of by the villagers. I spun to see a flaming redheaded girl, one arm folded angrily across her chest while the other held a cigarette at low level. Unusual for this industry, she looked younger than me, but she had a face that suggested she'd lived most of it scowling.

"There's a plane waiting. Let's go." I had no idea if the plane was for her to go, someone to arrive, or for me to escape the rather hallucinatory day I was having.

She then gave me a pointed grunt, and tapped with her foot at a suitcase that I hadn't noticed until then, clearly expecting me to load it for her.

"Hi! I'm Peter!" I tried to make friends again.

"Nice for you," she said, drew harshly on her cigarette and waved in the direction I should go as I threw the suitcase in the back. It was a mercifully short drive to the airstrip, and we made it in a frosty silence.

There was a plane there, the pilot grumpy because I had no water for him.

I suddenly realized that I was about to be left alone at the airstrip, and really wasn't sure that I'd be able to find my way back to the camp. But I immediately felt my spirits rise again. I rarely met people I didn't like, but this girl was one of them, and she was about to leave. Not only that, this country was already providing me with challenges I'd never have faced if I'd stayed in the suburbs. This place felt untamed. The redhead swiveled, her movements jerky and chicken-like, threw her cigarette to the ground, crushed it, and swiveled on it once, made a face like she'd licked lemon, and handed me some keys.

"You'll need these," was all she said.

"Um, thanks," I took them, careful not to touch her fingers in case they were poisonous. "So, who's the manager back there?"

She just cocked her head at me, and I started to believe that this too was some universal gesture, probably for "You're an idiot," that I had previously never known.

"You are," she said, and got into the plane.

I'd never managed a camp before, and never met the staff of this one. In fact, I wouldn't know where to find them if they chose to hide from me, because I'd never been there either. As I watched the plane take off, I suddenly wanted her back.

Welcome to Botswana, I thought again, and started making my way along my tracks back to the camp.

THE WATER WAR

I lasted only a few days at Duba before I was whisked off to Savuti Bush Camp, as they were desperately short of a manager there.

"Um," I had feebly protested, "I'm not a manager."

"Just for a little while you have to be," I was instructed by Alan over the radio, and being new with the company didn't dare argue, or point out that in my first few days at Duba the staff had taken advantage of both my naïveté and my preference for being liked at the expense of being respected.

After a short flight it was with some trepidation that I was picked up by a smiling Motswana at the airstrip, and he told me that it would be a forty-minute drive back to the camp as the track was very sandy, and we'd probably get stuck. This, I imagined, must impress arriving tourists enormously.

"So you're a guide here?" I asked, hoping not to have a repeat of the performance by the staff at Duba, where some had claimed to be a barman one day, a chef the next, and just a passer-by visiting a friend when I had asked them to do some work.

"No," the man answered, "I'm a tracker." He then started showing off his knowledge by naming the trees we passed ("*Lonchocarpus nelsii*," he said proudly, "also known as the Kalahari apple leaf!" and beamed), and in the interest of polite banter I asked why he wasn't a guide yet.

"Ah!" he replied, high-pitched and righteous, then "Ah! Ah! Ah!" again, clearly ready to express some indignation, "they won't give me a driver's license!" and with that we promptly got stuck.

"I can't imagine why not," I commented, as he aggressively revved the engine, throwing sand in a high arc onto me and my luggage and digging us deeper. I wanted to tell him some of the little I had learned about off-road driving, which was that in sand the instant you have no momentum, accelerating is useless. Only digging by hand works. But he was so enthusiastic in his foot pumping, and I lacked any assertion, so I resigned myself to the inevitable and jumped out to get some branches.

"Wait!" the tracker shouted as I took a few steps into the bushes. "Check for elephants!"

The bush was sparse enough for me to see some way through it, so I made an exaggerated effort of peering through it. The tracker clambered from his seat and onto the bonnet, using the height to see farther than I could. "The elephants here are baaaaaaaaaad!" he explained, "not like the ones in the Delta."

"Okay, there are none, let's go," he announced, and with his all-clear we searched for branches to use as ramps, wedging them under the tires once we had jacked them up, me using the heavy lifting implement very cautiously as I always did, my scarred head throbbing at the sight of it. As we worked, the tracker explained that the elephants here were desperate for water. We were far north of the Okavango and its aquatic riches, and the Linyanti River was several miles away from Savuti. The elephants passing through were sometimes insane with thirst, and could be extremely temperamental.

In the camp I learned just how bad it was with the elephants. The place was a mess. The surrounding bush had been decimated by the thousands of elephants that gathered here each year as the Kalahari dried, and the camp looked almost destroyed.

Everything was patched or panel-beaten. A war was going on, and the humans were losing.

The outgoing manager explained to me that along the dry river bed that the camp fronted were four water holes, each of which had water pumped by a diesel generator, the old-fashioned sort with a heavy cast-iron handle that you cranked to start the machine. I was warned that if these weren't run regularly and the water holes were sucked empty, the elephants would come into camp and wreak havoc.

"Easy," I thought. "Just run the pumps."

What I hadn't factored in was the amount of maintenance needed to keep a camp presentable. My workload was greater than other camp managers' because I had no idea what I was doing, and was likely to take something slightly damaged and in my attempts to repair it, break it completely.

So the next day I set out to Manchwe Pan, a water hole named after the occasional ostrich that was seen there, and parked by the water hole. It was dry, nothing in it but some crackly leaves and dust. I hauled out a jerry can of diesel and a funnel, and crab-walked under the load to the generator. It had a cage around it, shoulder height with a corrugated tin roof on top. The cage was a response to inquisitive baboons that stole the heavy belts that drove the flywheels, just because they were fun to play with.

I flicked open the sliding bolt, and lifted the diesel to start filling the generator's tank. Bent almost double as I was to fit inside, it wasn't an easy task. The cage was designed by a midget, I was sure, as there was no way a human of normal proportions like myself could fit inside comfortably. With my neck sideways and my back finding every screw in the tin above, I filled the tank, and grabbed the heavy handle to attach to the crank.

It was impossible to turn. My arm wasn't long enough to crank start from outside the cage, and inside the midget's torture chamber was an impossible working environment. Contorting myself further I gave another turn as best I could, a feeble effort that barely made the generator cough. I tried again, still twisted, before a voice in my head gently suggested, "Squat down, you moron."

My knees crackled viciously as they bent, a legacy from being the world's worst rugby player for many years, and with my improved posture, I was able to give a heartier turn with the handle. Some enthusiastic burblings came from the machine, encouraging me. Another shoulder-wrenching heft, and I was rewarded with the cage filling with an oily black smoke, but the gennie didn't come to life quite yet.

Along with my wounded knee, I have a shoulder that never healed from a running injury. This already ached from the exertion, and I was getting grumpier every minute, cursing my broken body, my uncoordination, and the midget cage maker. But I tried again, one turn with some violence to it, and kept going with the handle, building some momentum, and the machine kicked into life, filling the bush with a resonant *tock-tock-tock.* I groaned as I stretched my knees slightly, and planned on backing out of the cage, when over the sound of the generator I heard a branch snap.

Suddenly I felt very vulnerable. Most of me was in the cage, but I was presenting my protruding backside to Botswana, and wondered what was out there. Peering between my ankles, I saw tree trunks everywhere. Too many. Some of them moving.

The elephants' superior hearing allowed them to pick up on my first few attempts to start the generator, and they had swarmed from the bush. I couldn't believe how many had appeared in the few minutes I had been laboring, and how many more were still arriving.

Or how far away I had parked the Land Rover. Between me and it were at least twenty-four legs, and there was no way I could get to it without being squashed. The blood was running to my head, and I couldn't leave my butt hanging out in the world, so I made an awkward swivel and sat inside the cage, wondering what to do.

For a while my grumpiness disappeared as I enjoyed my unusually low vantage point watching the elephants, all bulls, that shuffled and grumbled and slurped around the spout that splurted water into the shallow concrete pan. Occasionally a shoving match would break out between two of them for the best position, the elephants (usually known as ellies) savoring the clean water straight from the spout rather than what was in the pan, already muddied by the toes of their fellows. Two combatants came dangerously close to the cage, and I wondered if it wasn't going to end for me right there, but they swerved off, tusks scraping against tusks as they shoved heads, before they realized they were missing out on a drink and scurried back to the spout.

While I can never get tired of watching elephants and their interactions, I was becoming numb in my cramped quarters and the diesel throb was not my preferred soundtrack. At first I wondered how long I might be stuck there, before realizing I held the power. "Moron!" I insulted myself again. "Just switch off the bloody pump!" With no water the elephants would move on to whatever business they had been taking care of when they had heard the generator, and I could bring the Landy closer to the cage and fire it up again.

My finger wavered at the kill switch, not wanting to go through the excruciating gymnastics needed to start it up again.

Faced with the alternative of hours in the cage, I hit the button. With a reluctant sputter the noise died down, the body language of the elephants immediately showing disappointment. With shrugged shoulders and flaccid trunks they stared at the spout for a while, as if they could use strength of will to make water appear from it, before slowly and silently disappearing into the surrounding bush.

I sidled warily from the cage and fetched the vehicle. This time I parked it hard up against the cage, offering me shelter for when the elephants came back. They returned in even greater numbers as soon as they heard me cranking, perhaps wondering what all the words meant that I was shouting as I did it.

It took me many more goes to get it started this time, and I was purple, sweaty, and trembling by the time it finally chortled into life. The impatient elephants trumpeted as the water finally trickled out, as if to say, "Finally!"

"These ellies are trying to kill me . . . " I muttered to myself, but of course was wrong. Something else entirely would try to do that.

◉

"Ko-ko!" the woman's voice said, the Motswana's way of saying "Knock knock!" I ignored it as best I could, burrowing my face into the pillow.

"Mister Peter! Wake up! There is no water in camp." I rubbed my eyes, as it seemed unusually dark, and I had been promised a sleep-in this morning. No matter how I rubbed them, though, it couldn't disguise the fact it was still nighttime. The clock beside me confirmed it was four-thirty in the morning.

Without moving from the inelegant prone position in which I slept, I suggested to the lady who had bravely made her way to my room that she should switch the pumps on, even if it woke the tourists. "The pipes are broken," she said flatly.

"Get Matengu to fix them," I said, naming a perpetually cranky staff member with an incongruous Hitler moustache, not caring if he was woken up.

"Mister Peter, ALL the pipes are broken!"

Grumbling, I rose, threw on some clothes and sandals, and muttered my way into camp.

The pipes *were* broken. All of them. I had been warned that if the elephants managed to drain the water hole they would sometimes enter camp, and push over one of the hot water tanks outside a tourist tent. This would empty out, and since it was connected to the main system that fed the entire camp, all fifteen thousand liters from that would also flood forth, and a new pan would form outside some sleepless tourist's tent.

Before I had worked at this camp, I had felt some uneasiness about the concept of pumping water for animals, and not letting nature take its course. But as wild areas have dwindled, animals have no option but to stay in places like Savuti, so we needed to provide for them. I was starting to resent that duty while looking at the fallen tank, its buckled stand, and the torn pipe work that I would have to repair. The damage wasn't restricted to this one tent, though.

An elephant had strolled in, found the water hole dry, and consequently resolved, "I'll just knock over one of those water-fruits, then," and finding the tank empty tried the next one, perhaps thinking "Huh! Who'd have thought they could all be dud!" Then moved to the next, and the next, knocking over all six tourist tanks, plus the one outside the kitchen.

I spent the entire day repairing pipes, and getting staff to plant sharpened branches like stakes around the water systems, knowing that sharp stones were enough to deter ellies in some places. It was exhausting manual labor, and by the end of the day I felt shattered.

The next day the tanks were over again, the elephants having simply kicked at the stakes the same way they removed nutritious bulbs from the ground. We made longer stakes, planted them deeper, and again I fell into bed that night wondering what it was about this job that had attracted me.

Normally I waited for the tourists to leave on their drive before I started the generator opposite our camp, not wanting to shatter the silence they had come to Africa to enjoy with its rude putterings. But I wanted the water hole overflowing that night, so much liquid in it that it couldn't be drained. I'd sent Matengu to pump water to the other holes as well, to ensure that every elephant in the area didn't feel the need to visit our camp.

The cage opposite camp had the same design as the other, but it had the advantage of being some distance from the water hole itself. There was no rush to get it firing the first time.

I warmed my shoulder up as I popped the bolt, and kicked my legs out a bit to get some circulation to my knees. Then I paused, standing for a moment enjoying the bush sounds, a distant fish eagle, a lark nearby, the clatter of zebra hooves as they made their way along the channel, and the rustle of leaves blown by the hot wind.

Swinging the cage door open I leaned in, trying a new technique, my backside once more to the wind but with my body arched so more stress was on my back and less on my knees.

It didn't work on the first go. The second was no better. After the third attempt I was forced to admit that I just wasn't getting enough leverage, and needed to squat. I started turning the handle while standing, and rocked forward on my toes as my butt came down to my heels. As if cursed, it was at this moment that a scorpion chose to climb my sandal, only to find itself threatened by a looming moon. And the scorpion did what scorpions do, planting its stinger and releasing a neurotoxin.

A searing pain erupted high on my thigh, sizzling heat like I had never felt before.

With an unmanly yelp I unfolded and launched upwards, immediately banging my head on the top of the cage, the blow sending me forward, reeling, wincing as my back scraped across the top of the cage door, tearing my shirt and peeling off skin.

I wouldn't have imagined that there were any more pain receptors available in my body at that moment, but that was because I hadn't fallen onto the drive belt yet, which had started whisking along at speed with the unintentional crank I'd given it. I fell onto the belt, losing skin from my belly to match my back, before scrambling off it and wedging myself into a corner, gasping and in shock.

In the opposite corner stood my attacker, his pincers held high as if in victory, his vicious stinger arched over his back, aimed at his vanquished foe.

Suddenly all of my fatigue from the past few days, all of my anger against the unwanted managerial position I was in, the anger against the elephants, and the midget, all my rage was focused on this tiny adversary.

A burning shot up my leg as I got to my feet, hunched and raw, and loosened the pliers-and-knife tool that all safari guides carry from my belt.

I don't believe in hurting animals unless it is in self-defense, and even then that it should be avoided if possible. I believe that animals feel fear and pain just like we do, so I can't abide trophy hunting, but right then I wanted that scorpion to die a thousand deaths.

Taunting me, it did a little jig as I inched toward it. As I drew my arm to strike, it reared its tail back, ready to hit me again. Like boxers we faced off, and then the scorpion made its move. With speed I wasn't expecting, the scorpion did something quite sensible, and scuttled under the generator, where I couldn't reach it.

"Coward! Bastard! Midget!" I shouted, and felt my rage dissipate with my silliness, as it usually does.

Battered and abraded I extricated myself from the cage, plucking my torn shirt away from the raw skin on my back and belly. In the distance I could see elephants scrambling down to the fast-filling water hole. This was a breeding herd, females and their babies, and even in pain I enjoyed their company.

Above them in a dead tree sat a fish eagle, which remained sentinel over that small patch of water every day. I'd been watching this bird, and had a theory that back twenty years earlier when this snake of grassland had been a flowing river, this had been its territory, and it had never given up hope of seeing it flow again. All it needed was some moisture to maintain that hope. As the pan filled, the eagle gave its famous call, and I was thrilled to have pleased it.

Still, if I had longer arms that scorpion would have been dead.

Nuts

To my relief the management positions I had been thrust into were short lived. I had "lost" the alcohol storeroom keys, it was raided, and the staff became incapacitated for two days, leaving me to make desperate pleas for help to the office in town. Soon after this a guiding position was quickly offered to me, to return me to my level of competence. And I wouldn't be guiding in just any old camp, but at Mombo, known as one of the best places in the whole of Africa to see wildlife.

The problem was that I appeared to be particularly poor at finding it. Unlike South Africa, I had no tracker perched on the bonnet to tell me where we were, spot animals, or direct me to the places that other guides had described on the radio as "pumping" with wildlife. I would hear them call in lions, leopards, cheetahs, wild dogs, and know that the tourists I led wouldn't see them because I didn't dare drive anywhere other than slow circles around the camp in case I never found my way back to it. "This is really good cheetah habitat," I explained to my tourists, peering meaningfully in all directions, but seeing nothing, really missing Titus.

I was having the slowest drive of a slow week, and had been out all morning without seeing anything more exotic than the plentiful antelope that could only hold people's attention for a few minutes before their grazing became commonplace. The tourists were bored. They, like so many others that come to Africa, wanted cats.

"Baboons!" I shouted, my enthusiasm for this common species greater than was warranted. Yet I did have a plan. Baboons are fascinating animals, active during the day. Best of all, the longer you watch them, the more they remind you of humans. The young play games like king of the mountain (or termite mound in this case), the adults squabble over meals, they flirt by raising brows, and if the tourists weren't the sort to be offended by their regular fornication, the baboons could provide a solid twenty minutes or so of entertainment before the tourists remembered they'd come to Africa to see lions.

This troop had crossed an open plain to sit around some fan palm trees, an island of vegetation only twenty yards by twenty yards in a sea of grass. The female trees were laden with heavy nuts, chocolate brown and heavy, almost the size of a tennis ball. Many of these nutritious nuts were scattered on the ground, a rare bounty of food available only because few species had the tools or teeth to eat them.

Some female baboons sat on the ground, vaguely watching their youngsters play at peekaboo or wrestling, as they used their enormous canine teeth to pry open their lunch. Other baboons had climbed the tall, single-stemmed palms, resting their calloused backsides against the thorny fronds and plucking nuts straight from the tree. The gusto with which they were cracking these nuts might have been why they weren't watching out as much as they should from their elevated perch.

One gave a truncated alarm bark, and I swiveled in my chair to see what he'd spotted, desperately hoping for some cheetah crossing the grassland behind us, or a leopard out way too late from its normally nocturnal activities.

But it was an elephant, a big bull, using a path that would bring him by our patch of palms. The baboons weren't concerned about him being predatory, as elephants are strictly vegetarian, but watched him closely because this was the only animal that could compete with them for the food supply they had discovered. The rifle-shot pops of cracking nuts stopped as all the baboons prepared to get out his way if he started feeding.

This elephant, though, seemed intent if relaxed about going elsewhere, his casual strides eating up distance.

"He might be communicating with other elephants," I explained to the tourists. "They have a language that is complex, but just too deep for us to hear. Most of their language is out of our hearing range, in the same way that dog can hear higher whistles than we can."

Again there was a mirror between baboon and human, as we all watched the elephant in a relative hush. Just as the baboons began to relax and I pondered whether it was worth following the elephant to see where he led us, he paused, one leg lifted, the lower joint giving a jaunty swing as its momentum carried it forward. Then he swiveled. He'd changed his mind. Wherever he was going was suddenly unimportant, and he felt like feeding. In two giant steps he was at the base of a particularly tall palm and rested his immense forehead against it.

A male baboon high in its branches started giving a deep booming alarm call, "*Boh! Boh! Boh!*" He knew what was coming, and so did I, already shaking with laughter. The elephant's body tensed, and with a violent shove he shook the tree, rocking it forward and smacking it with his head again on the backswing, sending an audible vibration along its trunk.

Nuts shook loose, falling like hail onto the bull's head, neck, and back. I'd seen elephants feeding like this before on palm and fruit trees, and their reaction to the pitter-patter of falling food was always the same, hunching up as if afraid something larger might drop. Perhaps the occasional branch did fall on them and it was wise to brace for it, but seeing an animal that is impenetrable to even some bullets afraid of a fruit pelting made me chuckle.

Not the baboon, though. The violent swaying of the palm he was trapped in had him in paroxysms. He screeched as if being attacked by a leopard. The elephant ignored him, and shook the tree once more, this time short sharp jabs that upset the baboon even more. More nuts fell, but clearly not enough for the elephant, as he gave another mighty shove, disrupting the small shakes with a blow that sent the whole tree swaying.

The baboon's grip, admirably firm until now, came loose at the toes, and his legs flung skywards, followed by a hand. Vicious curved spines on the palm fronds may have helped him hang on for a little longer, but with another shove he was dislodged and plummeted, a Valkyrie howl as he fell.

It was a long drop, and I don't imagine a human would have come out of it in a state of good health, but despite being stronger than any human, a baboon is lighter and it was with only a mild thud that the animal landed.

The baboon's blow was softened somewhat because he didn't hit the ground. He landed instead on the elephant. While braced for the nuts, the elephant seemed completely startled by the weight of the fruit he'd dislodged, particularly when it grew legs and ran the length of his back.

How the elephant had not noticed the howl of the baboon and made the connection of what it was that landed on him I will never know. But discrediting the intelligence I usually gave the species, the elephant acted like Chicken Little. With a squeaky trumpet he began galloping away before the baboon had reached his backside.

The rest of the baboon troop did something I'd witnessed baboons do when one of their troop was attacked by a crocodile.

With no way to help, they formed a cheer squad. As one they stood on their hind legs and screeched their encouragement, a cacophony of simian shouts that seemed to add to the elephant's distress as he picked up his pace.

The fallen baboon clung grimly on for a few seconds more, watching the ground rush by some distance below him, before deciding he had no career as a jockey and launching himself into space once more off the elephant's rump.

The behemoth trumpeted again but kept running, the baboon attempting to hit the ground doing the same, landing with legs moving, only to roll and disappear into a dust cloud.

As the air cleared he sat there, orange eyes wide between dirt-clearing blinks. The troop went nuts. Like a crowd at a sports match witnessing a miracle finish, they ran to him, shouting ecstatically and back-slapping the bewildered baboon.

And like fans waiting for the next thrill, they dispersed in short time, and went back to the nut stand to carry on eating. The last baboon sitting there was the one who'd survived two flights that day, and after a quick inspection of his limbs and a dust-off he trotted over to the food again.

Perusing the nuts on the ground, he evidently found none to his satisfaction. With some resignation in his posture, he climbed a palm tree and grabbed a single nut. Those around him stayed on the fronds, crunching into the hard kernels, but he looked out across the plain where a distant plume showed the elephant, still running, and climbed back down, and ate the nut on the ground. He climbed for another, and returned to the ground to eat this one too.

"The monkey's afraid of heights now!" a large tourist bellowed, and burst into laughter. Normally I would have asked him to keep his voice low, and corrected him on his species name, but let it pass as they were all enjoying themselves so much.

I looked at the small alarm clock I had wedged in the dash and realized we'd been with the baboons for over half an hour. I was almost late for brunch, where I knew the tourists from other vehicles would tell my group what they had seen, comparing and competing, even out here, just like baboons.

I knew what the other guides had shown their tourists this morning, and again mine had missed out on seeing lions, but for once I had a feeling they wouldn't mind.

SAD SNAKE

"Peter?" The voice was shy, hesitant. I did nothing but grumble in reply.

"Peter? Please ..." It was Yolanda, one of the camp managers, so technically now that I was a guide again I shouldn't have been doing my utmost to ignore her. Nevertheless I dragged a pillow over my head and wished I was deaf. In the camp hierarchy I was above the mechanics, the laundry ladies, even the chefs, on a par with the other guides, but had to answer to four camp managers. One was an old friend, Chris, who had given me my first job in the bush some years before and was now the overall manager of Mombo. He was assisted by Grant, like Chris a South African and veteran of the safari industry, and two female managers who oversaw issues like catering and supplies while the two men repaired things I had broken.

"Wake up!" Yolanda's tone had become insistent.

"But I'm not guiding today!" Since arriving in Botswana I had been thrown in the deep end—after my unusual job interview, and disastrous start with camp management, I had finally started guiding, but without any sort of break for more than a month.

Each morning my alarm would squawk well before the birds did. I'd stumble to my car and make sure I had no punctures, change the tire if I did, grab a coffee, wander the camp waking up guests and rubbing sleep from my eyes, perk up by the time tourists got to the deck, harangue them into the vehicle, watch animals for four hours, get back, eat brunch, tell stories, head to the airstrip as many as three times to pick up and drop off guests, drive again for four hours in the afternoon, sit for dinner with the tourists, tell more stories (hopefully not the same ones as at brunch), walk the guests to their tents, put the hyena-blocking gates in place around the deck, go to bed, and wait for the alarm to start it all again. Now, I finally had a morning where I wasn't driving, and Yolanda was insisting I get up. Grant, her partner, was kindly guiding on my behalf that morning, and I really wished he'd been around for her to pester instead.

"Why?" I asked, quite reasonably, I thought.

"There's a snake stuck in a tree!"

You're kidding me, I thought, and an involuntary sob of frustration escaped me. "Yolanda!" I wailed. "Snakes can climb trees!"

There was an offended pause. "This one's stuck."

"Buggershitpisswee," I muttered, threw on some shorts, a hat to cover my mad hair, and stomped out. "Where?" I asked curtly, wanting to show I thought this a fool's errand.

Yolanda led me to the area between the office that she manned for much of the day, a reed structure that was ready to collapse with the first strong wind, and the main deck. In between them was a rain tree, a slender-trunked tree with pale bark mottled in various shades of gray. This particular example grew at a steep angle, chasing the sunlight blocked by the thicker-stemmed ebonies that grew nearby.

I hadn't been exactly right when I had shouted that snakes could climb trees, because some of the thicker-bodied adders were strictly terrestrial. The snake that had Yolanda's concern, though, was a python, perfectly capable of getting up and down anything arboreal. When I saw this one I stopped, rose to a level of wakefulness considerably greater than earlier, considered an apology to Yolanda, but just said, "Oh."

Instead of the usual round trunk, this tree was unusually box-shaped, as if begging to be cut for lumber. About halfway to the tree's canopy, on one of the faces perpendicular to the ground was a fist-sized hole. From this, hanging vertically by its head, was a python at least nine feet long. Its entire body hung straight down, the tail tip about four feet from the ground.

The python must have been investigating the hole for nesting birds, nocturnal mammals snoozing, or squirrels in hiding when its body somehow lost its grip and it fell, its head getting stuck like a key turned sideways in a lock.

Either that, or it had only just noticed that it had no legs and had decided to kill itself.

The snake moved, and I felt a rush of urgency. I ran to it and grabbed the tail, setting off quite a thrashing. The python was without a doubt still alive, and determined to stay that way. I was ready to do everything in my power to help it, and tried lifting the part I could reach, hoping it would give enough support for the snake to get its head out.

Clearly, though, the python felt I was threat, because it flailed away from me. "A ladder! I need a ladder!" Some of the African staff had started to gather to watch.

"Why is Peter fighting the snake?" I heard one of them ask.

"Not fighting! He's trying to get it out of the tree."

"Why? Will he eat it?"

"Maybe. That Peter! He's crazy!"

While these speculations and libels were being spoken, I was trying to climb the tree, figuring if the python could do it without limbs, it should be easy for me.

Nope. I fell out, my feet sliding on the smooth bark, my hands strengthless after too long gripping nothing but coffee cups and steering wheels.

A camp hand named Cisco sauntered up with a ladder, but in his inimitable style he had chosen the two-step ladder, the sort that is just dandy if you need to reach into the back of your kitchen cupboard, but no good when you are on a snake rescue mission.

The python's movements were slowing, and I sprinted to the workshop and grabbed an extension ladder, ran back as best I could with it, and spent precious moments trying to get it steady on the uneven ground. It was rickety at best, made worse by the shakes I got as soon as I was above the second rung and my fear of heights kicked in.

The hole the python hung from was about thirteen feet from the ground. I had placed the ladder too far from the snake, and had to reach far across to get to it.

I grabbed the snake, and it moved less vigorously this time, just a shrug, as if admitting defeat. I pushed up as hard as I could, so all the snake needed to do was unhook its head. But it couldn't, or wouldn't. I had to let it go. As gently as I could, I took the weight off it, the same weight as a young child hanging from that thin neck, and shimmied down the ladder, reset it directly beneath the snake, and raced back up, the snake draping over my back. Using my shoulder to support it, and both hands riskily off the rungs, I eased it free of its prison.

The python was dead. I am not sure at what point it died, or exactly whether it was a broken neck (which on a snake is rather long) or suffocation. I don't know if I could have helped it by being any faster, but felt some guilt that I hadn't left bed sooner.

I brought the snake down, its slick skin on mine, cold and rubbery. I sat with it, and coiled it up like it was still alive. I was feeling grim, with a headache starting from not having had a coffee. It felt like it was going to be a bad day.

There was a chirruping from the tree that had been the center of all the drama, and from the same hole that the snake's head had been in a tree squirrel emerged. She held a baby in her mouth, still pink and furless. In a few dainty bounds she carried it to a different hole, higher in the tree, on a thinner branch. She returned for another, another, and another. I imagined the terror of a sinister reptilian head invading your home, and threatening your babies, teeth as long as your body exposed with every tongue-flick. I looked at the dead python, whose simple existence had ceased just trying to make a living. Like so many animals, and almost as many people in Africa, survival for the snake, and the family of squirrels, was on a knife edge.

I decided that my morning wasn't that bad after all.

SPEAKING MONKEY

It was a book! One I hadn't read five times already, like all the others in camp. And I had three full hours in the middle of the day to get into it, no airstrip pickups, drop-offs, or walks to take. I had hovered over a tourist as she grew closer to the end, like a vulture over a dying animal, willing her to finish before she flew to the next camp and my opportunity for entertainment was lost. My room had one sagging bookshelf, mainly wildlife texts, but also what fiction I could scrounge when opportunity presented. Books were heavy, therefore difficult to transport in the weight-sensitive light aircraft we used as ferries. For me, a lifelong reader, this dearth of material was one of the few things I disliked about my way of life.

I clutched the book to my chest as I scurried to my room, waving to the workshop guys who were repairing a broken-down vehicle. Their shirts were off, maybe the last month they would work that way before the winter chill set in. Even here in the Kalahari some winter days were cool enough that you layered up and never stripped down.

Now, though, it was warm enough for me to leave the door to the canvas-and-pole structure I called home open, allowing what small breeze there was to circulate. I peeled my shirt off, and tossed it into the corner. My sandals were kicked in the opposite direction, and in nothing but shorts I flopped onto my single bed and opened to the first page.

I was about ten pages in, enjoying myself immensely, so thoroughly engrossed that I was undistracted by the sounds of squirrels racing each other across my roof, birds scratching in the dust by my door, or the distant mutters of the workshop guys cursing something or somebody. The squirrels stopped racing, and one set up an insistent chirring. Then another joined in, a repetitive noise, the sound of someone spinning the pedals on a bicycle, over and over. *"Chirr, chuck chuck chuck! Chirr, chuck chuck chuck!"* The noise quickly becomes boring, then an irritant. I looked through the translucent roof of my dwelling, a tautly stretched plastic tarpaulin. While I did not trust the fidgety squirrels much when it came to judging what was worth panicking about, it was possible that there was a snake nearby causing their distress.

None was visible, a relief because I had made an inadvertent snake trap a few months earlier in the insane October heat. With a vast sea of silicone I had glued a capped PVC pipe through the roof of my dwelling, in the hope it would allow some hot air out. In hindsight it was entirely predictable that monkeys would yank it out as a curiosity and leave me with a hole that any clumsy creature could fall through, landing beside me on my bed. I wasn't lonely enough to consider a snake good company. The squirrel darted forward and peered in at me through the hole, screaming his furry little head off, as if to warn every animal in Botswana, "Look out! There's an idiot down there!"

"Bugger off!" I shouted at the squirrel, just wanting to read, and made a lame kicking gesture that wouldn't have fooled anything with a brain larger than a snail. The squirrel screeched, the bird outside my room kicked at dirt, and I heard a monkey.

"Kwe!" it said, then feeling it hadn't made its point strongly enough, said, *"Kwe kwe kwe kwe kwe kwe!"*

I sat up, trying to determine where the sound was coming from. More monkeys had joined in, and the squirrels and birds added their voices, a cacophony of alarm.

Leopard.

Nothing else would get this reaction, and while the wild-life books on my shelf might stress that the leopard is primar-ily nocturnal, in Botswana we saw them often during daylight hours. I grinned, happy for two reasons—while my reading was disturbed by the ructions going on around me, the monkeys in camp were nothing but trouble and I liked that they were being harassed. I was also delighted because a leopard active now, this close to camp, should be easy to find in the afternoon.

I figured it must be one of Nicky's kids walking around out there. We knew all the leopards in the area, their territories, and quite often the intimate details of their lives. Nicky was a favor-ite of all the guides, as she was a prolific mother and, atypically for her species, she was not at all shy. Her last two litters had been raised close to our camp. If Nicky wasn't shy, these cubs were bold. Her latest young were now just over a year old, and were spending more time away from their mother. There were two of them, a male and female, exquisitely marked and sure to draw gasps of admiration and awe from any safari-goer.

The little female was already showing sharp hunting skills, and I had seen her catch lizards, birds, and even a fleet-footed genet. Her brother, however, was not so instinctive, and had the poor habit of flicking his tail excitedly as he approached poten-tial prey. Which in his case was often something along the lines of a butterfly, not very nutritious or worth the effort it took to stalk. If it was him wandering around out there, the monkeys may as well have been laughing, but his sister might just give them something very real to fear.

After some minutes the noise died down somewhat as the monkeys moved off, not willing to be part of any young leopard's training regime, and I went back to my book, my eyes starting to droop from the fatigue of the day, the cover sagging toward my chest.

The bush was silent, lulling me to slumber, but for once I wanted to resist and enjoy my book. I forced my eyes open, stretched my jaw, cleared my throat, and caught some movement by the open door.

With no hesitation, no sign that this was unfamiliar territory, a leopard came into my room.

Immediately I knew that I had been right about it being one of Nicky's cubs, but it no longer looked as young and cute as when I'd seen it from a vehicle. If it was the male, I had a feeling he'd just scoot from the room as soon as he saw me, but as it came further in the delicacy of its features confirmed it was the little girl. I hadn't moved, just watched her over the top of my book, willing my muscles not to twitch.

This was not an animal I had ever feared, even when I had seen them at night while walking back from the main area, alone and on foot, in the hours they usually hunt. There was just a lack of menace from Nicky and any of her young that made them feel like family.

On the other hand, I had never been trapped in an enclosed environment with one of them, and places like Rudraprayag and Panar flitted through my mind, where notorious leopards had killed not just a few, but hundreds of people over a short space of time. They were both in India, to be sure, and African leopards tended to be underachievers in man eating, with the record being from Zambia at a measly sixty dead. Still, I had no desire to get this girl's score rolling, so I maintained stillness as she came further into the room, three graceful paces, and sniffed at the shirt in the corner. Maybe I imagined it, but she seemed to wrinkle her nose. "Must get that washed," I thought.

Then she turned and looked at me.

This was one of the many situations that I had never read a thing about how to deal with. Keep eye contact and risk threatening her? Look away and make myself vulnerable? I aimed for something in the middle, glancing at her over the top of the book, then nervously averting my gaze, glancing back, away. She just stared, perhaps wondering if I was flirting. To be honest, I'd had daydreams of attractive females entering my tent uninvited, but they had always possessed fewer spots.

Finally she'd had enough of my flickering eyes and turned, casually making her way back to the door. When just her tail was visible she paused and gave it a flick, as if to say, "Pah! How boringly you live!" and left. A bird squawked at her, the squirrels began again, and I wondered if she wouldn't come back in just to enjoy the quiet.

But she didn't, and I went back to my book. This time I didn't have any difficulty staying awake.

THE WRONG ELEPHANT

C amp management was a job I rarely enjoyed. Most days were spent repairing things the tourists had complained about, and any spare time was spent patching up stuff on the verge of falling to pieces. But Linyanti Tented Camp, or L.T.C. as we usually called it, was different. It was old-fashioned in style: plain A-frame tents, on the ground, no raised walkways, no elevated dining area, just dirt paths linking the accommodation in one of Botswana's wildest places. People relaxed more in these informal surrounds, and demanded less. Normally I protested when told I had to take a sabbatical from guiding and manage a camp for a while, but not when it was L.T.C.

I liked it here. My pulse stayed a few beats higher at L.T.C. The dense bush could, and often did, hide large animals that would appear in the beam of my flashlight as I cautiously escorted tourists to their tents at night.

The blood positively throbbed in my ears, though, when a vehicle driven by Conrad, one of the overland guides, came steaming back into camp only a few minutes after it had left. He was ashen behind the wheel, and the tourists sitting in the back were all clinging at their armrests, their faces set in a communal rictus.

"Oh my God!" Conrad exclaimed, flapping his hands at me, "there was a great big ellie, she came out of the feverberry bushes, flattened one, and then just tusked the car, again and again!" Conrad had a flamboyance that would not have been out of place in musical theater, but I could see he wasn't exaggerating this time. Water tinged a sickly green by anticorrosives bubbled from two brutal holes in the radiator, and the hood had deep gouges where tusks had slid along it.

Conrad's guests were persuaded that such a thing was unlikely to happen again, and after I'd given them a less-fractured vehicle to ride in, they ventured once more into the bush. Many times in my career I had persuaded guests their fears were unfounded, and done so with conviction. This time I almost crossed my fingers as I said that the elephants here were safe.

This camp was not in the Okavango, but beside a river in the far north of Botswana. If I threw an apple from the main area it would hit Namibia, as it was only yards away on the opposite bank. It was rare for me to throw anything, though, as I spent so much time here in a good mood.

The section of Namibia to the north of us was only a thin strip, beyond which was Angola. Elephants had been poached there for years, as the ivory could fund the purchase of weapons for their long-running civil war. Elephants fled from the area, going back only in desperation to feed their families. They took this risk because the Linyanti area was running out of food. In the dry winter months it becomes the only source of water for many miles around, and as many as sixty thousand elephants gathered along its banks to drink, stripping the vegetation until the landscape was barren, creating desperate times for every living thing in the region.

Some of our elephants were stressed through hunger, some also had experienced the deaths of their family members at the hand of man, and I imagined it was one of these that had done the damage to Conrad's front end. There was no malice in her actions, just a desire to protect her family. But a lack of malice didn't make the elephants any less dangerous.

It was only the middle of the dry season, but I knew already that this could become a very rough year. The river was low, the vegetation sparse, the elephants stressed. The next day Conrad would leave, and I would be taking guests into this environment. I wasn't sure how well it would go.

Yet I had an uneventful trip the next day as I drove to the camp's distant airstrip, and hoped my luck would hold. "We've just come from Xigera," the English guests replied when I asked where they had just been. "Spent lots of time on the water, we're looking forward to spending some time on terra firma. See some big animals and all." The Americans who had been on the same flight, and had come from the same camp, nodded their assent.

"Oh goody," I thought, but just giggled nervously. "Sure," I said, and an elephant charged out of the bushes. It barreled past us, head held high, doing the sideways quickstep ellies do when they wish to intimidate but have no desire for conflict.

The tourists all squeaked in unison, and I calmed them by explaining the situation with our elephants, and why some of them were a little testy, and that we might see a few more cranky elephants on our drive back to camp.

"But it's safe to be here, right?" the American man asked.

"Sure," I answered, as another elephant trumpeted nearby, a high peal that made us all jump. "Hopefully there won't be too much more ruckus before we get you there," I said, but there was. L.T.C. is at least forty minutes from the airstrip we used, if you drive at a speed that lets the bumps loosen your kidneys. It takes an hour driving at the pace used for tourists, and half that again when elephants appear from behind every bush with intent to squash you. Five times on the trip back elephants came at us, mainly mock charges but at least one that I wasn't sure enough about for me to put foot flat to the mat so we could rattle our way out.

In camp, after offering drinks and a cool cloth to wipe the dust from their brows, I suggested to the tourists that we might skip the drive that afternoon, and as walking was definitely not an option, asked would they be keen on yet another boat ride.

"Very sensible idea, that!" said the English lady, clearly terrified of our terrestrial beasts. "Lovely birds, I imagine," her husband added, as if concerned he would seem unmanly not facing the elephants. Again the Americans concurred, so I topped up the tank on the little tin boat, wiped down its seats, packed a cooler box with drinks, and we set out, upriver toward King's Pool camp.

It was a sedentary putter, far more relaxing than the airstrip transfer had been. Zebras picked their way nervously to the water, choosing a place with open ground to escape to if a predator appeared, while the leaf-eating kudus chose a place that had concealing vegetation. Elephants were less selective, not worried about lions or anything in the water, calmer here by the cool river than they were in the dry bush. Occasionally a crocodile's eyes would appear at the surface before sinking with a sinister slowness, allowing our boat to pass over.

I sped up only occasionally, to skirt pods of hippos that might see our journey as an invasion into their territory. Sometimes in the forest to our left an ellie would trumpet, and many made their way to drink from the water that we drifted upon. Overall it was peaceful, and from my position at the back of the boat I could observe the tension draining from the tourists.

"Put your cameras down now, please," I instructed everyone, "or we'll all get arrested." I saw the tension slam back into their postures at my cruel trick, so I calmed them again by explaining that the Botswana Defence Force had a small base on the river to stop poachers from coming across from Namibia. They didn't like photos being taken of their military encampment. While I felt seeing anyone else on safari fractured the sense of isolation, I was an admirer of the military's efforts in combating the ivory trade. We all waved to the soldiers as we passed their camp, the khaki tents blending well with the bush, while a soccer field with bright yellow nets at either end stuck out enough to blow any chance of meaningful camouflage.

Well before dark we stopped at a sandy bank, with a clear vantage point in all directions. While the tourists sucked at their gin and tonics before the ice could melt and dilute their potency, I downed water and sugary drinks, needing hydration and energy for the trip back.

I was about to begin expounding on the glory of our surroundings and its splendid isolation when the sound of a diesel engine crept into hearing range, then rapidly intruded. Being generally unable to locate noise, I peered in the wrong direction until I realized the tourists were all watching across the river. Two military vehicles were in a high-speed convoy on the Namibian side of the river, not pursuing anything or one that I could see, but clearly in a hurry.

Spotting us, the lead vehicle slid to a halt. The Linyanti is a not a wide river in many places, and as this was one of its narrower channels, if we turned our little boat side-on it would almost straddle the border entirely. We were doing nothing wrong, and were out of their jurisdiction, but I suddenly understood how an impala must feel when all eyes turn toward it.

"Is there normally this much military activity around here?" the American man asked.

"Nope," I said, "they might also be looking for poachers," I added, realizing that I was probably making this area sound like a hotbed of vice when moments before I'd been ready to start extolling its virtue. "And stopping fires," I added, "which is a good thing." I didn't like the way they were looking at us, though, so I packed up the cooler box and put it in the boat. Firearms make me nervous at the best of times, and two truckloads of men possessing them with no witnesses does nothing to improve my confidence.

I set us off on a slow putter again, and the vehicles shadowed us. We had broken no laws, and these were just young men in uniform having fun with the power they wielded, but unlike with animals I have little confidence in assessing human motivations. The tourists sensed my apprehension and sat with eyes left, watching the soldiers, as if they had been ordered to do so.

After a few tense minutes, with no fanfare the vehicles shot off, one driver giving us a lazy wave as they sped away, once more as if they had someone important to catch.

I poked my tongue out at them, a juvenile gesture to counter the subservience they had made me feel. I twisted my wrist a little tighter, giving the motor some more power. The sun was dipping lower, and I wanted to be in camp well before it set.

"You get lots of fires here?" the American asked, and I explained how they were often lit on the opposite bank by pastoralists. They burnt the grass in the hope of fresh green growth for their livestock, but these fires often escaped into the reserve opposite us, then jumped the river, fanned by strong, hot October winds.

"Last year I actually got caught in one," I began. "The fire had just hopped across, and any staff we could spare from all our camps formed a front to fight it. Even the army guys pitched in to help."

I was manning a point with Kevin, the overseer of all the camps in this region, in that fire. He was apoplectic, sure it was human failure allowing the fire to encroach. Soon it would threaten the area's largest and most expensively built camp. We spoke with our mouths twisted sideways as the air was thick with insects of all sizes, pelting us in their helter-skelter escape from the flames. If your mouth was open, they'd fly straight in. Winged termites tasted nutty, but wasps were no fun on the palate. Kevin raged that some of the staff just weren't paying enough attention and that was letting the fire get across. Just then we heard the *phffft* of ignition behind us. We were facing a wall of flame, still far enough away that we couldn't see any embers but close enough to tighten the skin and suck all the moisture from the air. Somehow, though, the fire was now also behind us, and I swatted at the small burning patch with a rake covered in palm leaves, a jerry-rigged fire beater that many others were also using.

"Turd!" I shouted at Kevin. He just ignored me, as most of the time I called him Fat Guy so a lack of respect was not unusual. He wasn't fat, but our mutual friend Devlin had insisted that he was before we met, and the name had stuck. (Devlin also told me once that a friend of his was so ugly that he had to be drunk just to look at him. His descriptions of people he doesn't like are even stronger.)

"Turds!" I shouted again, and swung my beater at another patch of flame that spontaneously erupted not far from my ankles. "It's the ellie turds!" I explained, "they're composting!" An elephant defecates as much as four hundred pounds of material each day, loaf-sized lumps of barely digested material that generate heat as they decompose. With the dry air and ambient heat around, the droppings near the fire front were erupting into flames without a spark, triggering greater and greater conflagrations. Kevin realized what I meant, no great intellectual leap as the lumps were burning all around us. We scanned our surrounds, and all I could think of was how much sixty thousand elephants spending six months of every year in this area would generate turd-wise.

"Crap," Kevin said quite appropriately. "Let's just try to protect the camp."

It was a close call, I explained to the tourists; the fire kept jumping across the tracks we'd hoped would act as fire breaks, and it took all of our efforts to beat out every ember that crossed and every dung ball that burst into flames. I'd never imagined that the most dangerous thing about an elephant could be its droppings, but we almost lost a camp that day, saved by a wind that turned the fire just before it hit the highly flammable thatched roofs. Not one of us came out unsinged.

"Do your parents mind what you do for a living?" the American lady asked when I'd finished telling them the story.

"Don't know," I answered, giving an ambiguous answer about my family as I always did, "but it is a safe job. . . . " I was about to explain my theory on this, that guides didn't get hit by cars, weren't faced with violent crime, and only had stress when leopards wouldn't show themselves, but stopped mid-sentence.

There was a herd of elephants ahead, and I didn't like the look of them. "More ellies?" the American man asked. "I can't believe it after this morning, but I think I'm getting a bit bored of them."

I would normally be offended by anyone describing elephants as boring, but in our short trip we had passed hundreds of them drinking by the river. This herd was twitchy at our approach.

"Those elephants don't look boring. We'll just stand down a bit to let them finish, then get back to camp." There was a definite shade of red in the sky, and once it seeped to gray we would be facing not just elephants but hippos as they became more active at night.

The elephants didn't like my plan and hung back in some thick blue-bush, huffing nervously. They had young ones with them, and I didn't want them to turn away from the river because of us. These may be Angolan elephants, and I thought it would be nice if for once a human showed them respect. So I let the motor push us further away, spinning it lightly every time the current pushed us to them, but they still wouldn't come down.

"Okay, I'm just going to cruise by as gently as we can, in the hope they stay around and drink when we pass." I explained my plans as often as possible to tourists so they would know that almost all my actions are meant to keep the animals relaxed. I throttled up, and the now-distant herd's trunks raised as one, sniffing the air.

The motor seemed far louder now that I wanted it quiet. It impelled us along at a gentle pace, the current with us, allowing me to barely twitch the throttle.

Despite my best intentions the herd wheeled, clustering protectively around the young, and moved at a swift pace further into the bush, some trumpeting their concern. I hated upsetting them, hated compounding any distress that humans had ever caused them, and was proud of the female that stood her ground and raised her head high, ears flared, acting as a shelter for the family. This was a common position taken by an "auntie" within a herd, holding the attention of something they perceived as a threat while the family went for safety, and I wasn't worried about her.

But I should have been.

She broke her pose and came right for us. I expected her to stop at the water's edge, but she didn't.

I thought the water would be deep enough to reach her belly and would slow her down, but it wasn't. This was the wrong elephant to try and sneak past.

Barely above her ankles, the water didn't change her speed at all, and this was no mock charge. Everything about her body language screamed that she intended to destroy us, and I twisted the throttle in my hand like it was a very bad chicken and I needed to kill it.

The boat shot forward, putting a little distance between us and the furious elephant. All four tourists were twisted in their seats, facing me at the rear of the boat, the fear in their faces telling me that I wouldn't have to explain to them to hold on tight and not ask for a photo. I felt spray on my back and glanced over my shoulder.

She was right there! Her tusks arcing, her bulk impossibly large. I felt like a fly when the swatter is coming down, and cranked my wrist further. Turning my head had shifted my posture somewhat, the movement transferring to my arm, which in turn pushed the tiller, which at this speed took us close to the bank.

"Don't look behind you!" one of the tourists shouted at me, his accent indistinguishable over the whine of the motor and the storm of four huge legs plowing through water right behind me. "Just go!"

I wanted to do exactly as the tourist asked, and just go, but loosened my grip. I will never understand why full speed on a boat motor can't be achieved within the normal limits of a human wrist. To get the last ounce of speed I had to briefly undo my twisted arm and hold the tiller with my other arm, before putting my dominant hand back and twisting until I hit maximum revolutions. The motor bit and we cut through spray, arcing away from the bank.

I looked again, and couldn't believe what I saw. Although she was now further back, she was still coming, her determination undiminished. She was scaring me. How far would she take this?

Then the motor on the little tin boat bit again, but this time not into water. The level of the river was low here, indicated by the choppy surface. I had stupidly not taken us by the deeper part of the channel. The tiller bucked in my hand like a living thing, jarring my shoulder and making my teeth clack against my tongue. Blood spurted inside my mouth, coppery and fresh.

Under normal circumstances I would reset the motor to a new angle until we were in deep water, but there was no time to consider the longevity of the propeller as it ground through mud and sunken hippo droppings, spitting them into a murky spray at the ever-pursuing elephant.

"Come on!" I screamed at the motor as we slowed to a near halt. I looked again and yelped as the elephant took the last few steps she needed before she could crush us at will. Even though I was standing, this was one of the lowest perspectives that I had ever viewed an elephant from, and it wasn't fun at all.

We got some traction in the water, the now-battered propeller gave us a shove, and we popped into deeper water, immediately gaining some distance from our pursuer. The tourists still sat like owls, eyes wide and heads twisted backwards.

The river ahead performed a graceful turn, curving around a low peninsula, before carrying on the near-straight course it would follow all the way back to camp. The turn was deep, and we could easily get past the elephant if she decided to swim after us, which I desperately hoped she would.

She displayed the intelligence that I usually admired so much in elephants and stopped at the turn. When the boat rounded the peninsula she would be there in a few short strides, right behind us again. Bugger. Why did she have to be so bloody smart? It was getting hard not to resent her persistence.

The first stars were beginning to appear, and hippos started calling to each other up and down the river. Soon they would want to get out of the water and feed, many of them cruising the channel to find a suitable bank to lumber out. We would be in their way, and a hippo's method of dealing with speed bumps is not a gentle one. So I powered up and started around the bend, the elephant giving a trumpet at the sound of the motor that made me jump and briefly lose my grip on the throttle.

The brief respite in engine noise allowed me to hear an exhalation, too hefty a sound to have come from any of the tourists. "Is that a hippo?" the American man asked.

"Yep," I said nervously. It was dark enough that I couldn't see it. Maybe it had gone under. Every ripple, every reflection of a reed or bobbing papyrus head was menacing. We were stuck. I briefly looked at the Namibian bank, just as a set of headlights came on. The army. If I decided to stop on that bank for a while they would see this as a threat, and no reasonable argument would work if they felt a bribe could be had. I had nothing to offer them except the tourists, and doubted I'd get much for them.

My options were between bad, worse, and worst. I made a decision based on mass. I pushed the little tin boat to its meager top speed, hunching low in the hope of offering less wind resistance and giving us a fraction of extra pace. The hippo reared ahead of us, gaping mouth showing his teeth, and splashed back down. The boat swerved around him, and I looked behind to see the elephant still in the same place, a front leg raised, as if she was ready to swing into action.

If she put that foot down, we were done for. I watched her intently, holding the throttle in a death grip. I was a great believer that in any crisis the wrong action can be better than none at all, but could be proved wrong if this elephant had enough anger to take a few more steps.

She planted her foot, I braced myself for the worst, but she wheeled and ran back to her herd, turning once to make sure we were still on our way. We were, and within moments were back in the safety of camp.

"How did you all enjoy your boat trip?" asked the manager as she walked toward us bearing drinks and flashlights, "Nice and relaxing?"

No one seemed to know what to say, until the American spoke. "Never tell this guy," he pointed at me, "that you think elephants are boring. He kinda overreacts . . . "

One of the "Beach Boys," who were the blonde-maned, dominant male lions from the south of Mombo.

The colony of cape fur seals on Namibia's Skeleton Coast numbered in the hundreds of thousands. Within the horde were always some individuals who slept so soundly you could play with their flippers and leave without waking them.

A typical early summer scene in the Okavango, my favorite place in the world and the only area where I feel truly at home.

This mature bull was relaxed even though I was lying in his path. Many elephants in Botswana allow a close approach because they have never been harmed by man. Others will flee at the first sight of a human, while a small few will chase you. As a guide, you quickly learn how to read an elephant's body language and pick which animals you can safely approach.

We knew many of the animals in the Mombo region by name. This was Nicky's son, whose name was eventually abbreviated to Nixon.

An African Wild Dog—the continent's rarest large predator yet statistically its most successful hunter. Stats aside, following them on their high speed hunts is one of the greatest thrills a safari can offer.

A guest tent at Linyanti Tented Camp. It was one of the few places I was ever content managing, despite the occasionally terrifying onslaught of elephants and hippos.

Dopey was a magnificent looking lion, but the only one I knew to chase his tail, or to try climbing palm trees.

As a child I knew that I was afraid of heights, and while uncomfortable admitting any phobia, was glad to have only one. Then I met my first crocodile. Now I know that there are at least two things in the world that unhinge my knees with fear, sour my breath, and overwhelm me with an urge to squeeze my eyes shut and wake up somewhere else.

My driving is legendary. Sadly, though, the legends are about how poor it is. This is the very first vehicle that I ever got stuck, still within sight of the camp that I had just driven out of, in South Africa's Sabi Sands Game Reserve.

It is a myth that the ostrich buries its head in the sand, foolishly believing that if it can't see a predator then the predator can't see it. They aren't that silly. It would be just as foolish though to imagine that one would ever beat you at chess. They have a lot of neck to support a little brain.

Hippos aren't any friendlier than buffalo. In fact, they are often quoted as being Africa's deadliest animals. It may be an overreaction to tutu jokes.

With water scarce in the Savuti Channel, the elephants would lord it over any other animal that wanted a drink. This little guy may have needed to wait a few years though before commanding the respect he wanted.

Leopards are the most sought after sighting for many of the tourists who come on safari. They are elusive by nature, their markings allowing them to blend with a surprising range of habitats. At Mombo Camp in Botswana though we saw them often, and at times they dropped their shy act altogether and appeared in the most unlikely places.

The view of the Kunene River, the only water source for hundreds of miles. Even though I expected to see it, I was still awed by this ribbon of water through one of the planet's driest places.

This cheeky baby elephant charged my Land Rover, before deciding we were a bit too big. His squeal brought a teenage sibling to his aid, and it was my turn to make a quick exit.

One-Horn the rhino was as close to a gentle uncle as you could get in a three-ton, armor-plated, heavily weaponed animal. Yet he was the only animal I ever saw that managed to frighten Titus, the experienced tracker I worked with at Idube Camp.

The two cheetah brothers (originally three) who were the dominant males of the Savuti Channel for an unusually long period of time. I knew them for ten years, so much longer than any book would claim they could live for, let alone control a territory.

Normally approaching wildlife from the water is a relaxing experience, but when I tried creeping past the wrong elephant, it soon became a lot more exciting than I had planned.

It is hard to know if any animal ever takes as much pleasure from watching us we get from them, but there was a day when this fish eagle seemed quite pleased with me.

I have no natural gift for photography but was lucky enough to accompany some of the world's best wildlife photographers, many of whom were generous with their knowledge. Silhouette photography became a favorite of mine, and I often paired it with my favorite animal.

The nutritious and tasty nuts of the fan palm are savored by elephants and baboons, the only animals with the tools to crack them open.

Zebras move so far and so often that they rarely grew used to our vehicles, and I have thousands of photographs of their posteriors as they
ran away. This was one of the few individuals who ever posed for me,
distracted perhaps by a whiff of lion on the wind.

BUSTED

I rarely drove the Maun Road. It was wider than the other tracks we used on safari drives, because the trucks that delivered us food and fuel once a month used it, and their greater wheelbases leave deep furrows. The Land Rover would bounce back and forth between these ditches, angling to one side, then popping out and lurching to the other. This seasickening swagger was unpleasant for the tourists on the back, and also for me as I wrestled the wheel.

But cheetah sightings had been scarce for the last few days, and I had a hunch that I'd find some around Suzie's Duck Pond. This was at the outer edge of our driving area, the last turn off on the Maun Road before the long, long road to town.

My tourists had seen more lions than they should have to tolerate, particularly as the ones we had watched had done little but sleep. They had also had great luck with leopards, and even watched wild dogs heading out for a hunt. They were dream guests, greatly appreciative of all they had witnessed, even the somnolent lions, and therefore I wanted them to see all they possibly could.

Despite the absent cheetahs and kidney-battering road, I had reason to be in a good mood. I had a break coming up, precipitated by the vagaries of the Botswana Immigration Department. My visa would expire in five days, and I had to leave the country to get a new one. So I had been granted permission to make a visit to Johannesburg. To the relief of my bank balance, a friend had asked me to take her car down for the journey, which was far less costly than flying. Three people had asked for a lift, all were girls, and I was single. Anticipating that drive, I smiled as I swayed wildly with my tourists down the Maun Road.

As we trundled along, I checked the trees for leopards, the ground for snoozing lions, and through the bush for whatever else might be there. It took us only twenty minutes to reach the outskirts of Suzie's Duck Pond, a wide-open area dotted with low-growing thorny acacias. It flooded after each rainy season, leaving rich grass that attracted zebras, wildebeest, and impalas. These in turn attracted predators, and the open ground made it a perfect spot for cheetahs to use their speed.

It also gave us an unobstructed view of a vehicle coming toward us. The plume of dust ejected from its wheels looked like a brushfire, and the growl of its diesel engine ricocheted from the trees. As always all the guides had discussed which direction we would head, and none of them had come this way. One of the things I liked most about Botswana was the feeling of isolation in the bush. Many times the tourists I took on safari never saw another vehicle during their whole stay. Only on the rarest of occasions was our blissful solitude interrupted. I sped up, approaching the oncoming vehicle, planning to get off the Maun Road before we passed each other.

To my surprise, instead of carrying straight along the road to camp, the vehicle took the same turn I had, and followed. My heart gave a startled flutter, then settled to a beat faster than usual. This didn't feel right.

While Botswana is a stable country, with no history of coups, dictators, or large-scale civil unrest like many of its neighbors, I couldn't expect my tourists to know this.

"Is that a military vehicle?" one of the Americans asked.

"Yep," I said, feigning indifference. "BDF."

"BFD?" they asked.

"Nope," was my reply, but I wondered if this might not become a big deal of some sort. "BDF." I paused, and tried as casually as possible to look behind us, which is futile when your vehicle has no mirrors and you have to extend your head like an excited tortoise to do it. They were still coming, so I spoke some more to cover nervousness that was building like steam in a cooker. This didn't feel right. "It stands for Botswana Defence Force. A few years back the son of the former president took over the military, and sensibly decided that since any war Botswana was in would be in the bush, not towns, army units should patrol wildlife regions. He also said they could shoot poachers on sight." I glanced behind us again. They were still there, keeping pace, like a hyena behind a wounded animal. "That pretty much took care of commercial poaching in Botswana," I concluded weakly. My good mood was drowning under the weight of nervous anticipation.

I decided to force the issue, and stopped my car. I could see now that the BDF vehicle was also a Land Rover, not a game drive vehicle like ours but a pickup. The cab held two soldiers, who just stared at me as I got up from my seat and started describing some golden orb weaver spiders that had webs strung beside the road. I was just pointing out a different sort of spider on the web, and without my usual enthusiasm for obscure terminology was going over klepto-parasitism, when the soldiers left their car and started walking toward me.

"So what this little guy does," I carried on, while the soldiers listened politely, "is wait until this big girl catches some food. Then he twitches the web over here, and while she rushes up, thinking she has caught something else, he scurries around and eats as much of her food as he can before hiding in the outer reaches of her web again."

None of the tourists were paying attention, and for once I wasn't offended. The two soldiers, recognizing that my babble had finished, walked over and said, "Can we see your license, sir?"

Really? I thought. Really? Out here? Instead I stifled a nervous giggle and said quite honestly, "Well, I don't carry that with me."

"Ah!" the taller of the two soldiers said, a common exclamation in Botswana to describe shocked disbelief. "Ah!" he repeated, looked at his colleague, turned back to me, and said "Ah!" again, in case I had missed it the first two times.

"No really, I don't," I explained, ignoring the calm rational part of my brain that said, "Shut up. Say nothing. Talking can only get you into trouble." I rambled on. "It is a very important document, you see, and I wouldn't want it to get wet." It was a ludicrous statement, I knew as I said it. The soldiers looked at the cloudless sky, then back at the parched earth that clearly hadn't seen rain for months, and wouldn't for many more. Then looked at me, and the expression they wore overcame any language barrier we might have. They thought I was an idiot.

Instead of a sensible course of action, I started talking again. My mouth is perhaps my most exercised organ, while my flabby brain is rarely pushed hard, and is often left puffing and wheezing behind my jaws as they run, pleading for them to stop. Nervousness exacerbates my verbal leakage, and now I had a jolt of realization that made my tension worse. The soldiers weren't asking for a driver's license. They wanted my guide's license. Which I didn't have. Not in my wallet, nor in the camp safe. At all. The exam was only run every six months, and I hadn't had the opportunity to sit for it yet. So I flapped my lips at them some more, a cascade of meaningless words tumbled out, and I wondered if I should just start talking about the spiders again and maybe they'd go away. Instead I jabbered on about the deep respect I held for the Botswana Government, and that its documents were dearer to me than love letters or mail from grandma, and that I kept my license in complete safety, and finished weakly with "Yes! Complete safety! Back at . . . " I knew I couldn't say camp, because that was too close by and they could check, and Maun was only a radio call away, so I finished strongly with "I keep it safely somewhere."

"You must come with us back to the camp," the shorter one said, his face full of the seriousness that only a uniform can give such a young man. There were no guns in sight, and the situation didn't call for them, but there is a deep feeling of menace when the armed forces of any country start giving you orders.

"Sure," I said, and swung myself back into the car. "You can follow me, or I'll just meet you there." I imagined they would take the Maun Road into camp, a known entity to them, and avoid the messy cobweb of tracks that we used. I could lose them, take my time getting back to camp, and fulfill my obligations to the increasingly concerned-looking tourists.

"No sir," the shorter soldier said. "You come with us." Then he added more firmly, "Now."

"Sure," I said. "Sure," I added, trying to remain agreeable while concocting increasingly wild schemes to get away from them. "I can't leave the tourists here!" I finally exclaimed, hitting on the obvious. "They don't know the way back!"

"Ah! But sir! You have no guide's license. You cannot, under the laws of Botswana, drive them anywhere. Now come with us!" He stamped his foot, and looked young again. I felt I had an upper hand, and with my hands out walked the two of them back to their vehicle. "These people," I explained, "have paid thousands of pula to be here and see your beautiful country. Now what do you think they will say about Botswana when they go home if you just leave them sitting here in the bush? Hmm? How about I just drive them back to the camp and meet you there?"

"Sir, then we would have to shoot you." This was delivered in as casual a tone of voice as if he was telling me the time.

"Right," I said, feeling that was the most compelling argument they had given so far. "One moment, please, then I'll be right with you." Before accompanying them, I did have to take care of one thing. I went back to my vehicle, smiled as confidently as I could at the tourists, and grabbed the radio mike. "Base base base base, come in." The casual intonation I generally used when calling camp was gone. "Base base base base, come in," I repeated, and for the first time ever added, "Please." I looked back at the tourists, who were now muttering to each other in three languages, and gave them my very best attempt at a reassuring smile. I caught a reflection of myself in one of their camera lenses, though, and my pink skin was wrinkled in a frown which the smile only exacerbated. I looked like a walrus giving birth.

No answer came, and the soldiers twitched impatiently. I called again, and was answered by an English accent. It was Ella, a new manager and a potential flame for Chris. "Go Peter."

"Right. Ella. This is going to sound like a joke, but it isn't. I think I'm being arrested. Is Chris there?" There was a barrage of disbelief, my emphatic reply of time being something we couldn't waste, until Chris came on. "Where are your guests, and how are they?"

"Right here with me. And they're fine. So am I, by the way. You might want to get out here and drive them back to camp."

"Bit of a problem with that, chap," I knew what was coming, and didn't want to hear it, "my license is somewhere in Maun."

And so began a stand-off. I refused to leave the tourists by themselves in the wilderness, which seemed reasonable to me, but to the soldiers was a blatant defiance of their authority. In the camp a frantic search was underway for someone, anyone, who actually had their guide's license. Since no one could recall having ever been asked for it, those who had done the test had generally left the slip of paper wherever their homes were. The search in camp came up short.

Within an hour a plane was diverted to land at our airstrip, and met by Chris. A bewildered guide named Heidi who had been on her way to Victoria Falls was shanghaied and conscripted into service. I waved farewell to the tourists, spoke briefly with Heidi about what the tourists had seen so she knew what to look for, and was unceremoniously shown the back of the pickup. I climbed inside, grateful that I wasn't cuffed.

I shared my space with two elephant tusks. In the end of these was a cavity where a nerve as thick as a human's wrist had once been, now trailing some brownish ichor that I was sure I saw squirm. The cavities were stuffed with grass to diminish the aroma emanating from them. It was not very effective. I made my calving walrus face again, puckering like a maniac in an attempt to seal my nostrils shut against my forehead, and held the expression as the soldiers drove me back to camp, where I had a feeling Chris would be able to arrange my release from this situation. At well over six feet he had an awesome physical presence, and with a degree in industrial psychology he had the knack of persuading people to do what he wanted, without them disliking him for it.

My hopes were dashed once Chris put his negotiating skills

to the test, and was as ineffective at obtaining my freedom as the tufts of vegetation were at reducing the stink in the truck. "He is under arrest," the soldiers kept repeating, "and will be taken to Maun without delay to be charged."

In a sly aside, I reminded Chris that my visa ran out in only a few days, and asked if he had an idea how long the process would take.

"No clue. But don't worry, chap. We'll make a plan."

Who's we? I wanted to ask. I was the one being carted off to Maun. But Chris went back to making friends with the soldiers, as did I. In typical African fashion they switched from an impassive official mode to a chuckling bonhomie as soon as we made some jokes. They explained that a pilot had seen an elephant dead of natural causes, and as was policy they had been dispatched to collect the tusks, so they wouldn't enter the tightly regulated ivory market. This was a policy of Botswana's that I had previously admired, but was now less fond of.

Ronnie the barman gave me a small cooler box filled with water bottles for the six-hour drive, and Moosa the chef whipped up some sandwiches in the kitchen. She offered some to the soldiers, smiling flirtatiously at them. They giggled, and flirted back. Chris offered them beer for the drive, but at this they became all serious again, and hustled me into the back once more.

"I'll radio Maun," were Chris's last words to me as we sped off. I'd been given a bag with some of my clothes, none of my toiletries, and my passport with its soon-to-expire visa.

The soldiers drove like an enemy was behind them, rattling me regularly from my unstable perch on the wheel arch, chipping my teeth every time I attempted a swig of water to wash the dust from my gums. On the few occasions that they did brake for the curves, a blinding cloud of Kalahari dust would coat me again.

We were going too fast for a hat to stay on my head, so sweat ran down my forehead, mixing with the dirt to make muddy torrents that streaked my face.

It was in this condition that I finally met Trevor, in our company's office in Maun. The soldiers, to my surprise, had agreed to us stopping for me to get advice before I was charged. Trevor was the general manager of the safari company I worked for, making him one of the many people who outranked me. Since I'd been flung straight into the bush on my arrival, and he had sensibly been taking a holiday over Christmas when I arrived, this was the first time we'd met. It was not how I would have liked to make a positive impression with the man who arranged my pay.

"Any advice?" I asked Trevor.

"Keep your head low, mouth shut, and hope they let you off. Then get out of the country."

Great, I thought, and got back into the pickup, and drove to the army base. One of the soldiers accepted the bottle of water I offered him, while the other went to fetch his boss.

I was just weighing up whether I should be firm with this man, in a military fashion so he would respect me, or humble and obliging to show respect to his authority, when all thoughts were driven from my mind as he entered the room and sat opposite me.

He was a slightly built man, as most Motswana are, with close-cropped hair. His shirt was neatly pressed, even though his body language gave him every appearance of just having been roused from a nap. This seemed to have made him cranky. He stared at me, and I stared back, trying desperately not to focus on his most conspicuous feature.

He had the most mesmerizingly large nostrils I have ever seen. Massive, dark holes that flared outwards, and drew my gaze like a galactic vortex. On a normal-sized head they would have been deserving of a second look, but on his delicate skull they were no less attention-getting than if he'd had testicles for ears. I soon realized why they were stretched to such extremes as he began picking one of them with a vigor and enthusiasm so off-putting I had to shut my eyes.

"*Rra*," came a voice, and I opened them. The commander was addressing me by the Setswana word for "Mister." "You cannot guide in Botswana without a license." He smacked his lips grotesquely at the end of the sentence, as if delivering it had been delicious. "But," he continued, "these gentlemen are not officers of the Wildlife Department, and they should not have arrested you for this offense."

Suddenly I loved Captain Booger, and went to shake his hand before remembering where it had been. Instead I spoke, "So I can go?"

He laughed, a deep throaty chuckle for such a small man, "No," he said, "we will deliver you to the appropriate authorities, and they can deal with you." Suddenly he started shouting at the two soldiers, and I knew without understanding Setswana that they were getting a thorough dressing-down for waking him, a worse one for overstepping their jurisdiction, and I suspect another for not holding my eyes open while he did his gross finger dance.

The young soldiers hustled me from the room and I climbed back to my butt-numbing perch on the wheel well, while they drove me ingloriously through town. They kept shooting me apologetic glances, as if to say, "Well it was fine when we arrested you, I mean, we're just the good old army, those wildlife guys are plain mean." And I forgave them. They were just young guys, like me, doing their utmost to make a good impression on their employers, and like me, having it backfire as often as not.

Now I just hoped that the Wildlife Department could clear this up, so I could leave the country. I hoped it would be soon.

Not soon, I was assured when delivered to the next government body. The head of the department, a strikingly tall and handsome man, slammed his fist on his desk when the soldiers who had arrested me explained how they had caught this dangerous outlaw. "Bloody safari companies!" he exclaimed, wagging a finger at me. "They think they can get away with anything! Well, I'll show them!"

Oh good, I thought. I felt like a carcass that two jackals were squabbling over. "Any way that I can help, just let me know," I said, trying to endear myself to him, before realizing what I had just offered. He just sneered at me and started taking long strides from his office, which like most of the buildings in Maun was a prefabricated structure, low to the ground, that, strangely for a desert country, seemed designed to retain heat.

Like a scolded dog I strayed behind, not sure where we were going. He stormed into another office, snatched the phone from a startled secretary who had clearly been caught gossiping, and coyly admitted to me that the phone in his office didn't work. "Wolf," he barked at the caller on the other end, and I knew he was talking to Alan, the overall head of the company. "I've got Peter Bloody Allison here, you understand, and I am going to punish him, and you." There was the fuzz of a voice from the other end, words I couldn't make out. Joomo (for that was his name) looked slyly at me a few times and answered some questions that seemed irrelevant to me. "Young, yes," he said, followed by "like a monkey," then "in jail forever." I suspected he wasn't even on the phone anymore, but I hadn't met a Motswana yet with a sense of humor as weird as mine, so I acted suitably scared.

"Ha!" he finally shouted, "Still! He will be punished!" He slammed down the receiver, shouted at the secretary who just stared insolently at the two of us, and stormed out again. I walk fast by nature, but could barely keep up with his long strides. Back in his office he slammed himself into a chair, whipped his legs up, and thudded his boots onto his desk. Briskly opening a drawer, he extracted a book and banged it onto his desk. "G . . . G . . . Ah! Here it is! Guiding without a license! Now Peter Bloody Allison, let me see what I can do to you." His enthusiasm for his task and the vigor with which he attacked it would have been inspiring, if I didn't foresee it might end with me being drawn and quartered and fed on by Maun's army of stray dogs.

Joomo suddenly looked crestfallen. "Dammit!" he said, for some reason one of the worst things you can say in Botswana, and a word that must be spat out for real effect. "Dammit!" This time he shouted it theatrically at the heavens.

"What!?" I asked, just as loudly, caring quite deeply about his answer.

"I can't charge you! Dammit!"

"Excellent!" I shouted.

"Shut up!" he commanded. I did. "It says here the maximum fine here is two thousand pula, or two years in jail. That means it is a criminal offense, and I have to give you to the bloody police. One pula less, and you were mine! Dammit!"

Dammit indeed, I thought. Despite the obvious glee Joomo was going to take in dismembering me (or whatever he had planned), he had a likable flair to him. The police I had met in Botswana were humorless, keen to point out that I was white in a black continent, and unlike their colleagues in neighboring countries completely incorruptible. I'd been appalled by the open vice I'd seen in Zimbabwe but quickly learned that it was the only way a policeman there could feed his family. There was no way of greasing my way out of this with bribery as in the rest of Africa, and trying to would just submerge me in far deeper water. This occupied my thoughts as Joomo dispatched me to the police station, allowing me to walk there myself, "Don't try to run away!" He wagged a finger at me, "I know you now, Peter Bloody Allison!"

As I suspected, the police were not at all genial. "You have to stay here until your trial," they told me, and I looked into the grim cells aligned behind the policemen's desk. They were chock-full of drunks, and grim-eyed men with even less humor in their visage than the police. It did not look like a place I wanted to spend a moment, let alone however long it would take for me to be tried. "But our cells are full."

Relief washed over me, and it was explained that I would be under house arrest. Did I have a phone? they asked.

"No," I replied truthfully.

"Then where should we find you?"

I thought about it and gave the best answer I had given all day. "The Sports Bar," I said, naming one of the three pubs in town, a place that served a surprisingly good tandoori pizza. "I'll be there all night."

Maun is a brown town. Brown roads. Trees coated with brown dust until the rains come. Brown donkeys. Brown buildings making way to brown huts on the fringes of town. The monotony is broken by speckles of Toyotas moving on the roads, always white, always slow. The exceptions to the monotony are minivans that scream through the streets, haul over, disgorge a passenger, and scream on, driving like it is Johannesburg.

I waited there for my trial, sitting at the Sports Bar for four days, drinking with bush pilots, safari guides, boat makers, borehole drillers, the owners of stores that sold trinkets to tourists, taxidermists, medical personnel, the unemployed, the indigent, and others who made up the population of Maun, or Donkeyville as it is commonly known.

The three girls that I had been so excited about driving to Johannesburg with dropped out one by one. Nola with the lion's eyes was first, followed by Serena the shy English girl. I pleaded with Emma, also English, to wait a while longer, but she gave me the smile of a girl who is used to men begging things of her and flew away on Air Botswana. I'd had a powerful crush on her, and was now not only scared of my predicament, but resentful as well.

I had one day left to stay legally in Botswana. After that, when I departed the country and the officials saw that I had overstayed my welcome, I'd get a stamp that said, "Do not allow re-entry." That would be the end of my safari career. I had no home on the continent, no place anywhere to retreat to and regather. The only family I had was my sister, but she was far away. I'd probably have to go to Australia, the only place I didn't need a visa for.

Since I'd just been told by the company that I worked for that I would represent myself in the court case, not coming back didn't seem that bad. I felt neglected in my hour of need, and the joy I'd had on finally finding what I thought was a home had dissipated. Maybe I should just let the tide take me again, and see where I washed up.

Instead of waiting for the police to come to me, I visited them again, hoping for a court case, nervous that cell space might have opened up and they would enthusiastically offer me one to stay in.

"Your trial begins in one hour," the officer said.

"Thanks," I said, wondering what other charges I would have faced if I hadn't checked in.

The courthouse was an incongruous-looking building. It was low and flat for most of its span, but perfectly square in its dimensions, with a gently angled roof that kinked sharply into a Chinese-looking spire. Amongst the other drab architecture of the town, it was refreshing, but I sat nervously outside the room, wishing that I owned a collared shirt that didn't have the name of a safari company printed across the breast. I'd borrowed a shirt hastily, two sizes too large, unmatched to my khaki trousers and not fitting at all with my safari boots, with a ridiculously large collar last fashionable in the seventies.

I itched and fussed at my neck, rehearsing my line. "Guilty, Your Honor," I tried, hitching my breath at the end to suggest how distraught I was. I tried again, straightforward, serious, to show we were sensible men and that we should just get this over with. Many versions were tried, as I hoped that this would be the only time I ever had to speak the words.

I was told to go into a waiting room, where I sat feeling particularly pale-skinned. The closest to me was a forlorn-looking man from the San, or bushman tribe, his speckled head held low, hands wringing. I thought I recognized some of the hard-faced men I'd seen in the cells, but couldn't be sure. It amazed me that some of them were laughing and joking, as if going to court was a cause of no concern. I was more afraid of prison than I was of lions, elephants, or even crocodiles.

The men in the room grunted resignedly when called by a casually dressed bailiff. Four of the worst-looking were called at the same time as me, as well as the San man. I distanced myself from the dangerous-looking four, and stood next to the bushman, taking no pleasure from the unusual circumstance of towering over another grown man.

We stood in a dock together, with a crowd of people observing. Many seemed to have come for a picnic, and the smell of fried chicken and maize meal was cloying. The judge first read the charges against the bushman.

He read his name first, then announced, "You have been charged with the petty crime of theft. Stealing beer. How do you plead?" The bushman didn't seem to understand what he was being accused of, and the judge eventually said that he had pleaded guilty, but I wasn't sure he had.

Next were the four, and I pressed further against the rail, away from them, when they were jointly accused of theft, malicious harm, kidnapping, rape, attempted murder, and, drawing a gasp from the crowd, cattle theft. "You held a whole village hostage," the judge intoned, peering down his glasses at them, "this is a verrrrry serrrrious crrrrrime." Each "r" rolled like thunder from his mouth.

Then it was my turn. "Peterrrr Grrregorrr Allison," he rumbled, and so nervous was I that I said, "Guilty!" The spectators giggled, but were silenced by a stern glare from the bench. "What is this charge? Guiding without a license? This is a verrry serrrious crrrrime." Hang on, I thought. What the other four did was a verrry serrrious crrrrime! Surely I am nothing but petty? But I held my tongue, so flustered was I. "How do you plead?" I was asked.

"Guilty your sir. Your honor. Worshipness." I fluffed my line. The moment was too big for me, and I didn't like how amusing the gang of four seemed to find me. "Sir." I added again at the end, just for good measure. The judge gave me a look that I am familiar with, strongly suggestive that I should be scraped from the bottom of a shoe and the dog that dropped me be punished.

We were led back to the holding room, and I kept a hand protectively over my breast pocket, what was in it, and the heart behind it. The San rocked, and I wished I knew more than the word for "woodpecker" in his language so I could offer some condolence.

After countless hours we were led back out. The bushman was quickly told he was guilty, and given the option of a one-hundred-pula fine or a month in jail. He took the time, and I worried for him. The gang of four were also found guilty, and offered a joint fine of two thousand pula, the equivalent of five hundred dollars, between them all, or two years in jail. It seemed staggeringly low, and I recoiled from them further, even as they accepted the time, with stoic shrugs as if it was no big deal. Maybe for them it wasn't.

"Peterrrr Grrregorrr Allison," the judge said again, and now I thought he was maybe being a little showy with his big "r"s. "You are guilty of guiding without a license." Well yes, I thought, I've already said that. "Do you have anything to say?" the judge asked.

Many things to say flooded my brain, and as so often happens the flood was ready to burst the dam my lips had made and spill forth. For once, though, I would say nothing, and get into no further trouble. I was intensely proud to say, "No sir!"

"Oh, so you want the maximum penalty then?" the judge asked, genuinely quizzical.

"No! No! Sorry, excuse me, but really, I mean, no, I am very sorry, I didn't mean it, big mistake, never again," I babbled on, and again the crowd chuckled at this crazy white guy who had sweat marks from his armpits to his belt.

"Well then, because you are young, I will be lenient." Oh good, I thought. I knew the maximum fine was two thousand pula, or two years in jail. "So you can have four months in jail." Oh crap, I thought, and immediately started planning a dash for the Zimbabwe border, figuring I could live off the land, or bloody well learn, because there was no way I was going to prison. But the judge wasn't finished. "Or four hundred pula. Which would you prefer?"

"I'll take the four hundred pula, thanks, Judge," I beamed, like the winning contestant on a game show, and whipped cash from my breast pocket. I'd been given the maximum finable amount by Alan, and had guarded it jealously until now, and I waved it at the judge, not thinking how ridiculous I must look. The crowd laughed again, I saw the covetous looks from the gang and shoved it back into my pocket.

"You don't pay me," the judge said, probably wanting to add the word "moron," "you pay at the office."

"Okay," I said brightly. "Okay," a little more hesitantly, "where's that then?" The crowd seemed to think this was the funniest thing I'd said so far, and now that I wasn't going to jail I beamed at my audience, thinking how nice it would be to take them on safari since they were so easily amused.

"Out the door, turn right, right again, second door on the left."

"Thanks, Judge," I said, found the door to the dock firmly locked, provoking more laughter from the crowd as I rattled it, and at a nod from the judge hopped the railing and walked from the room a free, if confused man. A secretary looked at me with disinterested eyes, "Eh, *Rra*," she said, but reluctantly, as if the last thing she needed was to be bothered. This is the reaction from most of Botswana's civil servants, but today I was too relieved to be offended.

"I'd like to pay a fine, please."

"Eh *Rra*."

"There's nobody next door."

"Eh *Rra*."

"Can I pay here?"

"Eh *Rra*."

"Very good then. You'll give me a receipt, right?"

Wordlessly she reached into a drawer and pulled out a book with ragged sheets of carbon paper between its pages. "Eh *Rra*." She said, "What is the fine?"

"Four hundred pula," I said, counting out the brightly colored notes as she wrote the figure in her book.

"And the charge, *Rra*?"

"Murder." I said, as casually as I could. She began to write it down, but I stopped her, "No, no, no, just kidding. Only four hundred pula for murder? Really?" She just stared, unamused, far tougher to please than my courtroom crowd. "I am guilty," I took my time over the wording now, "of guiding without a license." She again looked at me with what I initially thought was disdain, but then I said, "Oh sorry, G...U...I...D" and she dutifully spelled it out, crossing out the word "murder" roughly, taking my cash and handing me the receipt.

I left the room, left the building, and later that day left the country. I wondered if it was worth my while returning, new visa or not. I liked the people I worked with. There was a feeling of risk, though, in living there, as if anything could happen, and probably would. Everyone had told me that no one they had heard of had ever been arrested in the middle of a game drive. No one else I spoke to either had a receipt for murder.

I weighed my options. Leave Botswana, and I may as well leave Africa and pursue the "real job" that most guides were avoiding, probably back in Australia. Or go back, and see what else Botswana threw at me.

It wasn't really a hard decision at all.

EXILE TO AN ISLAND

It seemed a silly place to put an airstrip. It ran right through the middle of a village, and like every village that I had seen in Botswana, this one crawled with goats and donkeys, animals with little respect for the threat an aircraft might pose.

As we buzzed the strip in a small Cessna the livestock did not move from their position. We banked, and through the side window I saw two small boys emerge from huts and start chasing the animals.

"Ah good, the Donkey Deceptors!" said the pilot, a friendly man named Neville.

Of course, I thought to myself, the Donkey Deceptors. It just added to the rather strange time I'd been having of late. After my arrest, and the trial, I'd fled to Johannesburg for some rest before coming back into Botswana. I'd been informed that I couldn't go back to Mombo for a while, until I had my guide's license. This had apparently never been an issue before, and I wasn't glad to have been the trailblazer.

"We'll send you to Jedibe Camp," my boss told me. "You can hide out there for a while."

"Hide?" I enquired, not relishing the idea of breaking any more laws of my adopted home, but my question went unanswered, my boss moving onto other things.

So now I was being exiled to a camp that sat on a small island in the Okavango Delta. The island was in fact so small it could not accommodate an airstrip, so one had been built nearby. The pilot shouted over the noise of the propeller to me that the two boys were paid a meager sum to chase the donkeys off the strip each time a plane was coming in. Once they had completed their task, our plane swung around, lined up, the engine note changed, and we bounced down, spitting dust, and taxied to a shady spot under a sausage tree.

The tallest Motswana I had seen so far emerged from behind the tree, wiping sleep from his eyes. With no preamble he flung open the door, and greeted the pilot loudly before turning to me. "Jackson! ATC!" he barked, beamed a huge smile of strong-looking teeth, then shoved an enormous fist into the plane, clutched my hand, and shook it vigorously, only letting it go after I gasped.

"Air Traffic Control," Neville confided from the corner of his mouth.

"Of course," I muttered, and watched as Jackson started hauling my bag from the plane with the speed and delicacy of a wrecking ball.

Once my bag had been torn out, Jackson strolled with it to a small tin boat that was tied to a rough jetty on the other side of the airstrip. I scanned my surrounds. The island was long and narrow, most of it being taken up with the hard clay of the strip, the cluster of huts at the other end being the only raised feature apart from the tree that Jackson used. Now I spotted a handmade timber bench by the tree, with some lettering carved into it. Looking closer, I saw that it read "Terminal 3." Where the first two terminals might be was a mystery that I never resolved.

Neville was staying overnight at the camp as well, so his bag was also torn from the luggage pod, while he attached the plane to tie-downs that would prevent it from flying off on its own in a strong wind. I looked up at the hefty seeds that hung vertically from the sausage tree above, known to drop and concuss anything underneath, and wondered aloud if that was the best place for them to have installed the anchor points.

"That's not the last strange thing about this place," Neville told me, but before explaining further he gave a sharp whistle and shouted, "Mark!" A lightly framed but heavily tattooed man popped out of the little tin boat, startling me because I hadn't seen him there.

He and Neville exchanged pleasantries, and I introduced myself. "Hey," he said, and I gleaned that he was a man of few words.

We got into the little boat, which was moored in barely waist-deep water. With a practiced yank on the cord, Mark started the motor and with expert swings of the tiller and twists of the throttle turned the boat around in the narrow, reed-fringed channel. I watched closely, as I had a strong inclination that in this water-based camp I'd be asked to drive a boat soon.

"Ever driven a boat?" Mark asked.

"Sure," I answered, "but with a wheel, not a, um, arm, er tiller," I finished, not mentioning it had been years ago, in the broad, still waters of Sydney Harbour, and that I had displayed no particular talent for the activity.

Mark didn't answer, and I marveled how the boat shot through channels narrower than the craft was broad. The waterway was barely a foot across, but the bow parted all vegetation in our path, like a mechanical Moses. Aquatic grasses whipped its sides, and papyrus arched overhead, almost forming a canopy in some places. We burst into open water, and as Mark opened the throttle and we picked up exhilarating speed, a grin formed on my features. My tongue flicked out to catch some of the spray we were throwing, and I imagined I'd like this place.

This was part of the Okavango I hadn't seen yet—wide-open water, endless banks of reeds and papyrus, hidden crocodiles lurking, hippos snorting, jacanas delicately walking over lily pads, and the promise of rare animals like sitatunga and clawless otters to be seen.

Within a few short minutes we cut out of the main channel, through an opening in the papyrus I'd barely had time to see, and wound our way through yet another twisting snake of water framed by reeds. The lagoon we emerged into was a glorious, glistening blue reflecting the few white clouds overhead, a distant corner alive with flowering plants with musical names like *ipomoea*. On the far side of the lagoon from where we had entered, a long jetty probed its way from the land. A lanky but attractive woman waved enthusiastically and smiled broadly as we arrived, accompanied by one yipping dog, plus a smaller pooch that appeared too old to muster the energy required to react to our presence. Instead it just wiggled its nose at us, then presented its backside for a scratching as we docked. I obliged, and said, "Hi! I'm Peter!" to the tall woman, as always hoping to get off on a good foot.

"Aukie," she said, which was pronounced "Okey." My smart-aleck instincts kicked in, and I was a moment from saying "Dokey!" back at her, but left it at "Okay."

I was quickly shown around the camp, a short journey as it only contained six guest tents plus two more for the management. A small kitchen, office, and main dining area all overlooked the lagoon, and completed the island's habituations.

"No guests," Mark said simply, "let's fish." I was unused to the luxury of a camp with no tourists, and thrilled that for once I would not be thrown into the deep end of an unfamiliar environment, but not quite as thrilled about what he was proposing. Fishing, to me, is like skiing. I comprehend that there are people who love the activity with a passion, but have never quite figured out why. But again, I was new at this camp, so acquiesced with as eager a grin as I could manage.

"Fly?" Mark asked.

I looked at Neville. He was the pilot. I'd presumed we'd take a boat. There was lots of water around. "Oh got it, fly-fishing, right, um, no, I'll just use that other sort." So I was handed the other sort of rod, whatever it is called, and climbed back into the boat.

"Drive?" Mark asked me, and I politely declined.

I should have accepted. I needed the practice. It had been years since I'd taken the command of a boat, and my break from tourists was to be a short one. Mark explained that many people who came to Jedibe would be keen on fishing, and most of those would have heard of, and would want to catch, a tiger fish. "They're easiest to catch where two channels meet," Mark explained, the longest sentence I'd heard him say in the half day we'd now known each other. He had an easy cool to him, which, combined with his roughly drawn tattoos, convinced me he'd seen some sides of life that made anything in Botswana seem easy. I'd met many people over the years who tried to play strong, silent types, but it was usually an affectation. Mark's persona wasn't put on, so I was surprised when he spoke further. "The small fish get tossed around when the two channels meet, and the tigers are strong enough to swim in and nab them while they're disoriented."

"Great fighting fish," Neville joined in the lesson, and I was not thrilled to discover that even a pilot knew more than me about the area that I was about to become an "expert" guide in. "If you hook one they'll leap, splash about, really put on a show. Great stuff," he was beaming, clearly in eager anticipation of such an encounter.

"Frankly I'd prefer fish to leap straight to my plate and indicate where the best cuts of sashimi are," I stated, but didn't get a response.

Despite my lack of joy in swinging a stick to launch some string, then waiting, waiting, waiting, waiting, and calling it fun, I was quite content once the casting was done. The nose of the boat was tied to some papyrus, the current behind us lazily swinging it one way, then the next. A still patch of water across the channel from us held many lilies, and to my delight I spotted a lesser jacana, a bird I'd never seen before. Knowing that some people found birdwatching as perplexing an activity as I did fishing, I quietly enjoyed the moment while Mark and Neville fished, not catching anything they thought worth keeping. Soon after, we made our way back along the twisting, turning channels so I could get to know the camp and its staff a little better.

Aukie showed me how the tents were numbered (not in a linear way, but quite randomly, for no reason anyone knew of) and pointed out the tree branches stacked in a rectangle behind each tent. "The branches cover the septic systems," she explained. "A few months ago a hippo trod on the soak-away and fell in. Made a helluva noise. Not the easiest thing to get out, either; Mark almost died trying." She imparted this casually, as if rescuing an angry, excrement-covered behemoth was the sort of thing most people faced on a daily basis.

"We've got some tourists coming in tomorrow, but Mark has to go into town for a day. You're ready to guide them, aren't you?"

"Sure," I said, though I was precisely the opposite. In the past, being thrown straight into the deep end in every camp I'd worked at had perturbed me, but the fishing trip here had only shown me how large the gaps in my knowledge were. I didn't know my way around the channels. I didn't really know how to drive a boat. I didn't have a clue what to say to the tourists after my three bits of information about papyrus had run out. I realized that not knowing how little you know can sometimes be a good thing.

Mark accompanied me to the airstrip the next day, which was useful as I had completely forgotten how to get there. As the plane buzzed by, the Donkey Deceptors rushed out, screaming at the animals. Jackson emerged, rubbing his eyes, from behind a tree, and Mark handed me a key. "Gun safe," he said. "Keep an ear out for cows."

I had absolutely no idea what he was talking about. Cows? Guns?

"What?" I asked, trying his trick of pithiness.

"We got robbed by some cows once. If you hear them coming, have the rifle ready."

"Okay, I'll admit, that still doesn't make any sense to me."

Mark explained that not so long ago they'd woken to the sound of many cowbells and a chorus of *moo*. In the middle of this wild area a herd of cows had appeared, dripping wet, on their island. With flare guns normally used for emergencies, the Jedibe staff had managed to muster the herd back across the water to the nearest, much larger island. As they wondered what had caused the cows to undertake the risky swim past crocodiles, someone noticed the office structure was missing a wall. The cows had been a distraction, and some unseen thief had used their noise to cover the sound of him removing the entire safe that held tourists' valuables.

"A cowboy?" I asked with a grin.

"No," Mark said without a smile, and we left it at that.

Soon after, Mark departed on the plane, which had disgorged two tourists for me to collect. They were French, he a withered prune of a man with enormous fleshy ears, she a porcelain-skinned beauty many years his younger, with a soft accent that hurt my heart.

"Zis boat is small," he said disdainfully when he sighted the tinnie, most of the seating covered by their bags, which Jackson had randomly tossed onboard.

"Yes it is," I said, "so is the channel. The *Titanic* wouldn't fit."

Ignoring my sarcasm, the man made his way on creaky knees into the boat, assisted by his gorgeous young companion who demurely sat in beside him. I'd never understood how it was that aged European men were able to attract such beauty, where I could barely get the attention of a baboon. Then I looked at my dust-crusted feet in their old sandals, my rough hairdo cut by a staff member reflected in the water, and my half-tucked shirt, and saw no reason why anyone should find me attractive at all, and set my mind instead to getting back to camp.

The boat was facing the direction we'd come in, nose to the dead end of the jetty. Short of dragging it and its occupants across the airstrip, I'd have to turn it within the confines of the channel. Mark had done it with casual blips of the throttle and elegant arcs of the tiller arm, in three turns having the boat on its way. At my forty-seventh attempt, the propeller clogged with aquatic grasses, and the tourists were splashed with Delta water spiced with goat droppings. All the while Jackson watched on, giving me a smile that showed he knew just what a mess I was making. I thought, "Bugger it," and jumped into the groin-deep water, wincing at the cold. I manhandled the boat around until it was facing where it needed to go, rocking with violent spasms that I thought just might tip the old man in.

With the propeller finally cleared and the bow angled at open water, I fired up and drove us straight into some reeds. "Swing the arm left to go right," I muttered to myself, backed the boat up slightly, collected more reeds, and thought about telling the French we'd swim the rest of the way. Instead I untangled the prop again, and set off once more. The ten-minute trip took us much longer because of the many wrong turns I took. I did my utmost to maintain an image that all this was part of our sight-seeing, but desperation was creeping into my tone as I'd been forced to tell them two of the three things I knew about papyrus to fill the embarrassed silences, and would have little else to say on this evening's activity. I told Aukie that I'd embarrassed myself on the boat ride back, and really didn't know what I was going to do apart from point the boat and steer it when we went out in the afternoon.

"China," she exclaimed, which is a common South African-ism for "mate," "that's all you have to do! Look at where you are! What do you think you can say that will make it any better for them?"

My normal guiding style was to flood my guests with infor-mation, so much that their heads would spin with the incred-ible amount there was to know about this, my favorite place. But what Aukie said to me turned out to be some of the best guiding advice I'd ever been given. That afternoon I set out with the French couple, and peacefully puttered downstream. Every now and then when the reeds and papyrus opened up I'd shut off the motor and let us drift. The only sounds came from the gentle slap of water on tin, the peeping of hidden birds, and the slight breeze through the high grasses. It was blissful, and anything I said would have ruined it.

On the way back the sun dipped, and a pinging sound began, first in one place, then surrounding us, growing in intensity. The

Frenchman turned to me with a quizzical look, and I did nothing but smile back. "What is zis?" he was forced to ask.

"Frogs," I answered simply, overcoming my urge to give him the name of the species and the scientific nomenclature. He seemed to be weighing up whether I had just answered his question or called him a name, then nodded his assent, and we drifted home to be met by Aukie at the pier. When she asked how their afternoon activity had been, the man smiled widely, "*Très bon!* Eez beautiful!"

Mark returned on the same plane that took the tourists out, who by their accounts had enjoyed their time, even if South African wine was not anywhere near as good as that from France. "Doesn't offend me," I'd said as the old man scrunched his face up at the table wine, "I'm Australian."

"Oorztralian wine," he hissed, "is also gar-baaarzh." He pronounced the word "garbage" so sexily that I suddenly understood his appeal to the young lady.

Mark and I waved goodbye to them as the plane took off, then neatly stowed Mark's bags that were strewn willy-nilly by Jackson's rough handling. Mark watched without comment as I took what seemed a reasonable seven attempts to turn the boat, only once having to clear the propeller. I thought I'd made a vast improvement, but considering my starting point there was little chance I could have become worse.

"No guests tonight. Let's look for poachers. The chief told me he thinks there's one nearby," Mark said.

"Sure," I answered, even though once again I wasn't. "We'll take Taxi," Mark added, naming the small, more active dog on Jedibe. We set out, the dog manning the bow, Mark sensibly taking the tiller without asking if I wanted to drive, and twisted and wound our way through waterways in which I was soon lost. We passed islands large and small, skimmed over sandbanks, and startled crocodiles that were sunning themselves on the banks. Taxi barked at these, and I watched him nervously in case he foolishly decided to take one on.

After more than half an hour's travel we came to a long oval island. It was fringed with high reeds and papyrus on one side, tall trees on the other, and a single termite mound in its middle which sprouted a half-sized ebony. After docking the boat we walked toward this mound, and sure enough remains of a fire were visible, along with snipped-off wire ends, the mark of a poacher who had been setting snares.

"Let's walk around and see if we can strip any out."

The fire hadn't seemed that old, so maybe its creator was still somewhere nearby, resenting our intrusion in his nefarious business. I wasn't comforted by Mark grabbing the heavy-caliber rifle and bringing it along, as it made me sure he was thinking the same way.

As we walked Taxi trotted along beside, sniffed at some bushes, paused, then gave a big growl for such a small dog. I waited for the snick of a round being chambered from Mark, but Taxi just trotted on, his tongue hanging out as if to say, "Tricked ya! Nothing there!" Perhaps this was the bush equivalent of the stunt urban dogs pull by staring at a corner and barking as if there was a ghost.

We followed the island's edge around, collecting snares at the predictable places, hung by each path the hippos had made, which would be used by all the animals crossing to and from this island. These animals did not behave in the manner described in guidebooks, and while this island was barely larger than a football field, it would be the occasional haunt of elephants, lions, leopards, and even the normally hydrophobic cheetah.

The poacher didn't appear, and we would never catch him. This island was in a national park, and while it was illegal to set these indiscriminate snares anywhere, the punishment would be greater for doing it in a protected zone. Mark whistled to Taxi, and told him to head to the boat. Obedient, he streaked across the center of the island, and I set out to follow, Mark a step or two ahead. I wasn't paying any particular attention, but it appeared Mark was getting shorter. Then he disappeared, at least as far as the waist, falling through a crust in the middle of the island.

In this scenario a sensible person would recall old Tarzan movies and get a rope. A sensible person would not run toward the person sinking into the Delta because surely they too would fall through, just as I did.

I'd felt little but a pull on my shoes, then the ground gave way before my legs plunged into surprisingly cold water. My arms caught me, and I too was pegged waist deep, half on an island, half under it. Mark must have heard the splash, followed by my sharp inhalation, but as usual said nothing.

I kicked like I'd learned to do many years before as a child in swimming school, raising myself slightly, but as soon as I put weight on my hands to draw myself out, the ground beneath them gave way, and my upper body plunged forward, my head connecting with dirt, making an empty thud.

"The island's hollow," Mark said.

Oh good, I thought, otherwise it was my head that had made the vacuous sound.

"There might have been tree roots here at one point that rotted out, letting water in, or a channel has just punched its way underneath the whole thing and we're in a river."

I already knew that the Delta was in a constant state of flux. Islands could grow from something as simple as dirt piling around a termite mound, vast plains could flood because a hippo made a path that water soon followed, and deep channels could dry when their supply was blocked by clogs of papyrus and reeds. I knew all this but had never had such an unsettling example as having the earth beneath me collapse. Still, I stifled a giggle at how silly we must look, spurred by the quizzical look Taxi was giving us, tilting his head from side to side, then yipping as if to say, "Hey guys! Your legs fell off!"

I tried kicking up again, but once more my hands just plunged through. The crust was only inches thick, muddy and stirred by my activity so I couldn't see what was beneath.

"We shouldn't stay here too long," Mark said casually. "Might be crocs."

I flurried, bemused as to how he hadn't thought this information was more important than the brief geology lesson he'd given earlier, but my flailing got me nowhere.

I calmed myself, then launched up and sprawled on my belly, spreading my weight on the ground across my torso and outflung arms. With fingertip clenches and contractions of my belly I slid my pelvis from the mire, then thighs, until my legs broke free. Slithering like a worm, I made it back to the last place I'd walked without leaving indents, and watched Mark do the same.

We both reeked like a warthog's groin, and I didn't want to stand near Mark as the potency of our combined aroma made my eyes water. I'd have moved away from myself if such a thing was possible. "Let's go," he said calmly, as if this was an everyday occurrence.

"Sure," I said, acting as if it was for me too. We skirted the island's fringe, solid footing a sudden luxury.

"Guests tomorrow," Mark said, once we were back in the boat. "Big family, we'll both be guiding. Maybe you should shower tonight."

So the next day I found myself at the airstrip, and cunningly turned my boat before the plane landed to save myself the humiliation of having to try it with an audience. The two Donkey Deceptors, though, witnessed my multiple attempts. They found them uproariously funny and were distracted enough that the plane almost hit a goat, veering off the strip, then back just before it would have plunged into the Delta.

The startled family were herded to the boats from the plane, after a brief moment of confusion when they thought Jackson was stealing their bags. "Not stealing," I explained, "just roughing them up a little bit." They were Dutch, a nationality that normally understood my sense of humor, but they just looked at me like it was my fault that one bag had landed half in the boat, half in the water after a brutal heave from Jackson.

As we puttered toward the main channel to Jedibe, I began the standard patter guides use when first meeting guests.

"Have you been to Africa before?"

"No."

"Have you been to other camps before this one?"

"No."

"Anything in particular you would like to see while you are here?" This I asked with a ludicrous hope that the response would be "Papyrus," but instead the patriarch said, "Lions."

"Right," I answered, considering whether to tell them how strange it would be to see lions here. All the way back to camp they scanned the high vegetation around us, smiles flickering then vanishing every time the reeds moved, only for it to be a heron, or stork, but nothing with fangs. Back in camp the family was delighted that Aukie spoke Dutch, and I hoped that she would break the news that this was a water camp, a fine place for relaxation in boats and flat-bottomed canoes, but not a place to see wildlife. I have nothing against Dutch people, and have enjoyed the company of most I have met, but find their accent and harsh language off-putting. To me it sounds as if they are gargling herring.

I knew a very few animal names in Dutch, but I could make out a litany of things they *hadn't* seen: "*Fershnigger* zebra, *fershnooger* giraffe," they said, or something like it; "*Fershnugger* lion!" one wailed. Clearly they were disappointed with Jedibe already, something it was my job to rectify.

That afternoon Mark suggested that I take the family's two teen boys fishing, as I could do it just around the corner from the camp and have less risk of getting lost in the maze of water.

"Sure," I said, and tried to prime the boys for the experience. "We have the chance to catch some bream," I explained, "probably a few catfish, and if we are very lucky we'll get a tiger fish. That's the real prize. So, no lions I am afraid, but will a tiger do?"

"*Fershnooger*," they answered, teen resentment at my clumsy pun oozing from every pimply pore.

"Really, it's great," I explained, pretending I didn't hold fishing in the same low esteem that they apparently did. "Tigers are a great fighting fish—if you hook one they'll drag the line around, they'll jump, they'll dive, they're a . . . a . . . fighting fish," I repeated lamely, running out of descriptions as I really had no idea what I was talking about. Get me back to Mombo, I urged whatever deity might live in this area.

I had gained confidence in my boating, and gave the motor a few good revs on the way out, and took some sharp turns tightly, throwing an arc of spray in the air, something I knew the boys would enjoy. "*Fershnugger!*" I heard one of them say excitedly, and grew a grin myself.

Soon enough we reached the confluence of channels that Mark had taken me on my first night, and I dared not explore further as I had come to the realization that I could get lost in a shoebox.

The two boys had simple rods with a device attached that I had learned was called a spinner. It had a triple hook with a brightly colored piece of metal attached, the shape of a spoon's head, that rotated as the line was drawn in. With fake authority I explained that the boys should aim for the turbulent water. I settled in for a wait, knowing that fishing was mainly a game of patience. Yet when the first brother cast, he hit the frothing water exactly, and with nary a splash, no fanfare, drew in a tiger fish that placidly sat on the end of his hook. It flipped disconsolately in the boat, and I just watched it, not wanting to deal with its needle teeth. Fortunately the boy who'd caught the fish knew what to do and with some swift movements of his hands removed the hook, and with visible disdain lobbed the fish back into the water.

"Very unusual that," I said. "Tiger fish are really known as a fighting fish, much more spectacular usually, very violent, um, angry fish . . . " I tapered off weakly, really wishing we had some lions to look at that I could speak about with some confidence.

The next brother cast, his line making a graceful arc through the air, the whisk of the line off the reel pure poetry. He expertly let the spinner sink a little, and drew it in with even turns on the reel. As it neared the boat it became visible beneath the surface and I released my breath, quite thrilled that it had nothing on it.

Then from the gloomy depths came a flash of silver, striped with black. As the spinner left the water a tiger shot after it, launching itself at the bait, mouth agape, and landed more squarely in the boat than I had ever seen Jackson achieve when tossing luggage.

It flipped violently on the tin, showing the spunk its species was famous for. I would have been delighted with such a catch, as it seemed effortless and not as messy a procedure as having hooks and mouths intersect. But the Dutch boys seemed disgusted. Letting off a stream of what was clearly invective (one word beginning with "f" is distinguishable in most languages), they both vented their disgust, finishing with, "*Fershnugger fershnooger* 'Fighting Fish,'" the words spat out as glares were directed at me, as if it was my fault the marine life here was suicidal.

Please, I begged the gods again, get me back to a place I understand.

After a month at Jedibe news came through that a guide's license exam was scheduled for me, and I had to get into Maun immediately so I could take it, and return to Mombo. After a trip to the airstrip along now-familiar channels past now-recognizable plants and bird life, I waved goodbye to Aukie, Mark, and the dogs, all of whom I had grown quite fond of, and waited for us to taxi to the far side of the strip. But we didn't, and I queried the pilot on one of the few things I knew about flying.

"Shouldn't we take off into the wind?" I asked, indicating the wind sock which flared with some rigidity. Some of the pilots had let me fly the planes when no tourists were on board, and I'd been gathering what knowledge I could about aircraft.

"Oops," the pilot, a new guy I didn't know well said, then added, "Daisy."

My confidence in the short journey ahead of me plummeted. If he couldn't remember something as basic as taking off into the wind, how would he handle something more complex, such as landing?

"There are two potholes in this strip," he finally explained, "named 'Oops' and 'Daisy.' If you don't hit them at the start of your run, you'll end up in the river."

"Oh goody, that's fine, then," I said, and we powered up, hit Oops, bounced into Daisy, and popped from there into the sky. As the plane banked I saw Jackson heading to his tree, Mark deftly turning the boat, and water, beautiful water, sparkling in the slanted light of the sun, and felt a pang that I hadn't understood this place better.

The pang turned to full regret within a year when it was announced that Jedibe, our least-occupied camp, was not commercially viable and would be shut down. My time there had not always been enjoyable, or explicable, and many tourists had felt the same. But it was a place where cows could be accomplices to a crime, where you could fall through the earth, and where fighting fish jumped clean into boats. I never found a place as mad, as beautiful, or more exciting. In the years afterwards I traveled to many places, but never found anywhere with that combination. I never knew a place that was quite as African.

BABOON PEOPLE

"So, Giddy, you do know the way, don't you?" I only asked because we were sitting at an intersection, and Gideon, a guide at Mombo like myself, had hesitated when I asked him which way to turn. We hadn't even left Maun yet, and as it is a place of few intersections (and therefore few opportunities to get lost, one would think) we appeared to be off to a bad start on our journey.

I could have blamed it on our early start, the darkness still cloaking the town, but it was light once we left, and Gideon had grown up here. Perhaps that's why he doesn't know how to leave it, I pondered, and followed his unconvincing finger as it pointed left. He nodded emphatically as the vehicle swung around the corner, narrowly missing a goat that skittered in front of us. Gideon scoffed at it, or perhaps at the impertinence of me questioning his direction.

Normally when I came back from leave I was rushed straight back to camp, bundled into the first available Cessna, and tipped out the other side, straight into the arms of needy tourists. This time, though, I had been given a four-wheel-drive Toyota (the same model that had fallen on my head, which added to my concerns about the trip), fully loaded with supplies for the camp, and Gideon as a copilot. I admitted to not knowing the way, but was assured that my navigator did.

Gideon did not. We had left the outskirts of Maun and were heading to the buffalo fence, a sprawling nightmare for wildlife that was erected in 1967. Its aim was to stop cattle and wild animals from mingling and carelessly swapping diseases. Instead it had cut off the migratory paths of thousands of zebras and wildebeest, killing them in staggering numbers. From the buffalo fence we would follow a vague and unmapped series of tracks that should take us to Mombo. In a straight line the journey was only eighty miles, but the tracks rarely went straight. They swept around forests, skirted flooded plains, rippled through deep Kalahari sands, and every now and then dipped damply into deep channels. Sometimes these became deep enough to swallow vehicles whole.

It had once taken a supply truck three days to make the trip, so many times had it become bogged down in sucking sand or had its tires pierced by the short sharp branches of the sickle bush. The fastest record was five hours, and I had some aspirations to beat this mark. This seemed unlikely, though, as every time there was a fork in the barely visible tracks that we were following, Gideon would hesitate, look calculatingly at whatever trees or shrubs were around, scan the sky for vultures, and assertively point. I had stopped saying, "Are you sure, Giddy?" because he would always give me the same harassed look, as if to say, "You are not my wife."

I actually knew his wife, a pleasant but physically daunting woman who was roughly three times Gideon's size. He was a slender man from the Herero tribe whose not so distant forebears had fled from Germans in what is now Namibia. Locked in a time warp from the date of their exodus, Herero women like Gideon's wife still wore full Victorian dress, complete with an elaborate headdress and a bustle over their rump that exaggerated its proportions and gave the impression that they were breaking a constant stream of wind. For a Herero man there was nothing that would make him prouder than a suit, and I had a feeling that Gideon would prefer to be dressed in one of those right now, working as an accountant.

"Fence," Gideon said simply, and I saw it. We had been driving through Kalahari sand and scrub, the strong smell of wild sage spicing the dust that plumed around us. Occasional acacias offered shade, and weaver birds flew from these as we passed, pursued by Gabar goshawks. Sometimes a small antelope called a steenbok would spring away from us, its delicate back legs kicking puffs of fine sand as it went. On the other side of the fence was the Okavango, and I looked forward to water hitting our tires and the coolness that would accompany the green grass and deeper forests it held. The usual excitement I felt when returning to the Delta overcame my jet lag, and a feeling of homecoming I get in no other place settled over me.

We crossed through a break in the fence and a smile of recognition passed Gideon's face. Good, I thought. We'd flubbed it this far, but were making good time by the alarm clock I had wedged into the dash. We jolted and plowed our way through the soft sand, rattling the bags of flour and tinned goods that made up some of our cargo.

A small flock of extremely well camouflaged birds burst from the track ahead of us, and whirred away. "Cape turtledoves," Gideon said, as if addressing tourists. We had been chatting on and off up to this point, both too tired to maintain any topic for too long, and enjoying quiet time before three months of enforced cheeriness and banal chitchat at work. So I didn't bother pointing out that the birds were not Cape turtledoves, not even doves at all but the less common double-banded sand grouse.

We pushed on, and in the distance I saw a cluster of waterbirds, and knew we were on the Delta's fringes. The ground was firmer, sand and silt mixing for a stable base. We picked up speed, and the number of tracks that bisected or branched from ours grew fewer and fewer. The sun dipped, giving some relief to my sunburned hands and neck. A rear wheel hit a spring hare burrow and the vehicle jolted violently, jarring my back and making my teeth clack audibly. Gideon grunted, and suggested we slow a little. I complied, but my right foot almost immediately started pushing harder again. I still thought we had a shot at the record, then realized that the track was disappearing. It hadn't been well defined for a while, and the burrow we had just hit suggested that animals had had time to colonize it.

The Okavango has no maps of any relevance, because the shifting floods mean that tracks are wiped annually, and even the landscape changes with channels drying up or filling with no warning, flooding open areas or carving islands in half. A GPS could tell you where you were, and where you needed to get to, but not how to do it. Right now I would happily have taken any advice, even electronic, as the track just petered out. I stopped the vehicle in the middle of an open plain, displacing some zebras who snorted angrily and galloped away.

"No road," Gideon said flatly.

"Right you are there, Gideon," I sputtered as I turned the car around and started heading back to the last junction we had taken. I drove faster than was necessary, faster than was sensible, because I still thought that maybe we were not so far off track that we might crack the record.

At the junction Gideon nodded emphatically, and said, "Yes, this way," as if it was my silly fault that we had taken the other fork. So we trundled to the west, though I had a feeling based on the many times that I had flown that our overall direction should be more easterly.

Nevertheless, on we pressed, through forests where baboons boomed their displeasure at the interruption and where unseen leopards surely lurked, across plains where wildebeest and impalas grazed, through scrub where surly-looking warthogs dug for tubers and roots. And then the road ended again, abruptly, with no fanfare. The word "lost" was on the tip of my tongue, but I didn't want to broach it just yet.

Five hours had passed, and we weren't going to break the record, which actually made me less tense. Now that I had no aim but to eventually reach Mombo, I relaxed and took pleasure in the environment. I had no idea where we were in the Delta, but it had the usual remarkable diversity, switching from desert to swamp in a matter of yards.

"Coppery-tailed coucal," Gideon said suddenly, pointing to a bird as it ejected itself from a date palm. The bird was in fact a white-browed coucal, a cousin of the species he had named, but again I let it pass. "Don't get stuck," Gideon added. Coucals tend to live near wet places, and where we were about to drive had the smell of tannin and mud.

"I won't get stuck, Giddy, don't worry," I reassured, and slipped into a lower gear. We ground forward slowly, mud splattering over our heads and onto our cargo. I was increasingly glad the load had food in it, as I wasn't sure anymore how long this trip would take. A wheel slipped and some mud belched, a cavity made by some long-lost log as it decayed, releasing swamp gas and sucking us in. We still had momentum, but no steerage in the mire, and the rear wheel hit the same cavity, and held fast. With a gentle squeeze against the accelerator I hoped to pop us out, but the front wheels just dug deeper. I quit before we chewed even further into the mud, and wordlessly, with the resignation of two men who had been stuck many, many times, Gideon and I walked away from the car in search of logs to place under the vehicle and give us traction.

163

It took us two hours to free ourselves, and darkness fell. A bat hawk swooped overhead, something I was happy to see because it wasn't a common bird. "Dark chanting goshawk," Gideon announced, even as it devoured a bat overhead.

After the mudbath I thought of calling it quits for the night and waiting for morning, wanting a daylight perspective on our location. But I didn't want the embarrassment that would come if any search party was launched on our behalf. Impatience to be in camp won out, and we carried on. Termite mounds in the southern hemisphere grow leaning to the north, and as we passed these I could see that we were still heading west.

Then, to my surprise, there was a light. The flatness of the Okavango allows you to see for miles, and with the comfort of the twinkle ahead I drove a little faster. Another twinkle appeared, the wrong color to be fireflies, and I grinned. Even though the thought of a three-month shift ahead was oppressive, I loved living amongst animals, was great friends with my co-workers, and had missed them while away. Mombo was my home.

So my grin wavered when I admitted to myself that the road we were on was completely unfamiliar. If we could see lights, I should recognize the trees and even termite mounds around us. I passed them every day, and their forms were as familiar to me as the street signs and neighborhood houses are for people who live in the suburbs. This was not Mombo. There weren't enough lights, for a start. Poachers? I thought, but instantly dismissed it. While I didn't know where we were, it was definitely deep into the Delta, and poachers wouldn't venture this far, nor make a camp so conspicuous with paraffin lanterns festooning the trees.

"Baboon camp," Gideon stated, then added, "I'm sure," answering my question before I could ask it.

I'd heard of this place. It was somewhere near Xaxaba, which meant we *had* gone too far west. Three figures emerged at the front of the camp, carrying flashlights and standing encouragingly at the camp entrance in a welcoming phalanx, just like we did at the tourist camps. But these were researchers, here to document every waking moment in a troop of baboons. This was an ongoing study that had lasted for many years. I almost turned the car around and set off without even greeting them. This was for two reasons. I am a male, and like all males am intensely reluctant to admit that I am out of my territory, and therefore need directions. I'd rather sit on a termite mound and make chest-thumping threat gestures at locals than say that I have absolutely no idea where I am and ask if they could please help me. I'd also heard stories about this place, and the people who worked here.

The word was that these baboon people were pretty odd.

In fact, I had heard a story from my friend and mentor Chris about why there were three baboon people, in a camp originally built for only one.

It had happened some years ago. Apparently, a young American researcher had come out and taken over the center after the previous scientist departed. Each day he would trek out and join the troop in the place they had slept the night before, and spend the day monitoring them. He would travel by foot, relying on the baboons' strength of numbers and visual acuity to warn him of any predators that might be around. The baboons themselves did not view the researcher as a threat to them or their young, nor did he take their food away, so over time his presence amongst them was normal. Baboons are social creatures, and often give each a friendly pat on the back as they stroll by a troop member. They started doing this with the researcher as well, tapping him lightly and giving a friendly *hoogh* sound as they walked by.

Every four days or so, one of the light aircraft that crisscross the Delta as aerial ferries would drop food for the researcher at the airstrip, and, in need of human company, most times he would be there to greet the pilot. He also gave a daily "all clear" on a radio channel to the air charter company, who were contracted to make sure not that he didn't get eaten, but that if he did the appropriate authorities were quickly notified, for whatever purpose that would serve.

But they were lax, and many days went by without a radio check-in. An alarm was only raised when a pilot noted that he had just dropped off food for the third time without the researcher being there to greet him, and litter from the previous drops was strewn around the strip.

The panic would have been enormous. Whoever said there is no such thing as bad publicity has never run an air charter company. The university that was funding his research was also paying them to look out for him, and they had surely failed. There were many presumptions the charter company could make. He may have been bitten by a snake and spent days in agony before dying, or been eaten outright by a lion, hyenas, or a leopard while in his camp. He could have succumbed to something as simple as falling and breaking a leg, and, unable to reach the radio, may have just perished. Whatever the cause for his absence, he was surely dead, and they set out in a plane with the back row of seats removed in the hope of finding a body to bring back as some small consolation.

They found no body in the camp, nor anything suggesting

violence. Searching the bush nearby, they found the resident, habituated baboon troop. The troop said *"hoogh"* at them and carried on doing what baboons do—feeding, grooming, fornicating, disciplining their young, and snoozing in the afternoon sun. One of the *hooghs,* though, had a different pitch. It was not as deep, not as gruff, not as purely animal in sound.

It was the researcher. He had gone native, so to speak. Naked and staring, he jabbered at them, and would not be coaxed to return to Maun. He wouldn't speak at all, just made the same barks and grunts that the baboons made. Alone for too long, and perhaps fragile to begin with, in his mind he had become one with the troop.

And the troop clearly thought he had, too. For when the pilot and charter company representative tried to forcefully bring him with them, the larger male baboons, stronger than a human by far and with longer canine teeth than a lion, charged at them and forced them back.

This was a problem.

But it was also Africa, the land where you make a plan. Without the restrictions that hold first-world societies back, a scheme was hatched, and the next afternoon they found where the troop was settling for the evening, and as the animals nodded off fired a veterinary dart into the researcher. The baboons were too afraid to retrieve him when he toppled from his perch (they hate the dark—it is when their prime enemy the leopard has the advantage over them), and the researcher was dragged away from them.

What happened next to him is unknown, but it was rumored that he was sent back to California, either for treatment or, as some suggested, because behaving like a baboon there would be accepted.

⊙

Like a few of Chris's stories, it was perhaps too good to be true.

Nevertheless, it was now policy that researchers would not be left alone, or even as a pair, perhaps so a witness would be present if one researcher visited violence on another. It was decided that threesomes were required, because there was no way that could cause conflict, was there? This was something Gideon and I would now get to investigate as we drove into the research camp and were greeted by two widely grinning faces. The other face was dour.

"Hello," said the squat but erectly standing blonde woman, and gave us a cheery wave.

"Hello," said the robust, bearded man, in a deep voice, sounding deeply displeased.

"Hello," said the tall and gracile brunette, smiling.

"Hello," Gideon and I said back, and it felt very ritualistic, as if we should now exchange a secret handshake. We did not; instead we all stood around awkwardly for a while, except Gideon, who for some reason seemed to be enjoying himself.

"We're a bit lost," I explained, perhaps unnecessarily, as I can't imagine any other reason you would turn up there unannounced.

"Oh, very nice," said the blonde, which seemed odd to me, because as exciting as being lost can be, it is mostly frustrating, and rarely nice. She added, "We've just had dinner, would you like a drink?"

"No thanks, just directions, please," is what I wanted to say, but in the milliseconds it took to form the words, Gideon had accepted, and even placed an order for a St. Louis, the inexplicably named national beer of Botswana.

So we entered their little camp, an open-air structure that allowed the smell of the Okavango to permeate it freely—tannin-rich water, potato bush, and the occasional nutty stench from the feces of their research subjects. Ever keen to learn, I thought I would make the most of our situation and learn more about baboons from them, so I broached the subject. The brunette went to answer but was cut off by the blonde. "No, let's not talk about work. It's so nice to have company. Let's just talk like normal people." The brunette shot her a dark look, while I hid my disappointment.

"Okay," I said, and hastily sipped at my beer. There was an apparent tension between the researchers. We had gathered around a large rectangular table, the sort that could do double duty for dining or dissections. The blonde had sat herself firmly between Gideon and myself on a bench seat. The bearded man had sat beside the brunette, who had immediately stood up and joined us, sandwiching me between them. This meant four of us sat facing the man, as if interviewing him. He held his shoulders forward, and his bearded chin thrust out. He looked like the sort of man who started a lot of fights, but from the way his nose was squashed it appeared he didn't win many.

I just wanted to go, and leave these people to their social research.

Gideon's beer can rattled emptily as he drained the last drop. Yet again, before my brain could snap into gear, he accepted another, and without asking one was placed in front of me as well. It was awkwardly quiet. I had tried idle chitchat, asking them where they were all from. "The States," they answered as one, and I began to think they had spent way too long as a unit.

"So," said the brunette. "It's a long way to Mombo. Maybe you should wait for light. You could stay here." I looked at

Gideon, but he was staring at the fridge that held the beers, as if he might be able to will another into existence.

I started recalling every horror movie that I had seen. Strangers stumble onto a small isolated community of people who start off seeming nice enough, then quickly do their utmost to eat their visitors' livers, or something equally as unappealing.

The blonde slipped Gideon another beer. Damn her. Bearded man just harrumphed at the suggestion of us staying, as he probably didn't like being usurped as alpha male. Or only male.

"No thanks," I replied. "Very generous of you, but we should be off. Last drinks, Giddy."

Are you mad? Gideon's face clearly said to me. *They have free beer!* It was only then that I realized that while our cargo contained ample foodstuffs and fuel for us to have been comfortably lost for days if need be, we did not have a drop of alcohol with us. This may have been plaguing Gideon while we were off course, and perhaps why he hadn't complained at how fast I had been driving initially. The man liked a drink, and I was glad that I was doing the driving.

I went to stand, but a hand came down on my thigh.

"Stay," said the brunette, the quietest up to now.

"Stay," the blonde pitched in, and I was sure she had somehow squeezed closer to me on the bench.

"Whatever," added the bearded one, surprising me, as I was sure he just wanted us to leave so he could reclaim his harem.

"No," I said, and shuffled myself backwards off the bench, getting a small splinter in the process and hopping inelegantly as I looped one leg over, then the next, to extricate myself. "We really have to go."

Gideon slid his slight frame out as well, and our hosts stood.

"We'll tell you about baboons!" the brunette promised, an edge of pleading in her voice.

"Thanks, but we have to get to Mombo."

"Well, if you change your mind, you know where we are," the blonde added.

Not exactly, I thought, or we wouldn't have been here to begin with.

"Let me help you with some directions," the man said, taking charge. "So you don't get lost again." He finished with a patronizing smile.

What he was saying hit a primitive nerve. The reason men don't ask for directions is that it goes against all ancient instincts. If you don't know your way, it means you aren't in your territory. And if you aren't in your territory, you must be in someone else's. This is their place, they have fought for it, they roar within it, pee all over it, plant petunias, or do whatever else is appropriate for their species to say "Mine!"

The man started drawing in the sand with his stubby finger, an X for where we were, another for nearby Xaxaba camp, a distant one for Maun, and then he drew a long line between two of them halfway back to Maun. "This is where you went wrong," he asserted, "you should have taken the other fork." And then he bared his teeth at us again.

Bugger, I thought. On his hand-drawn map the turnoff was a long way.

I thanked him, climbed back in the vehicle, wishing I'd had coffee instead of beer as there would be at least another five hours' driving ahead of me.

"Bye," I said, and Gideon echoed the syllable.

"Bye," said the brunette.

"Bye," said the blonde.

"Good-bye," said the man, making me feel for the briefest of moments that he would add, "and good riddance."

⊙

We revved on, away from the baboon people, and once out of earshot, I asked Gideon if he had heard the story of the single researcher who had gone nuts. He hadn't, so I filled him in.

"I think they're going a bit crazy, too," I finished. "Maybe three people together won't work either."

Gideon just humphed, as unimpressed by the story or my analysis as I was with his navigation. "They seemed like they wanted us to become part of their troop," I added. Gideon gave me a disinterested look in reply. Maybe such speculation was not something Herero did.

We drove more than an hour, into the darkness, our world nothing more than the stars and what our headlights illuminated. We hit a deep, crosswise rut in the road, and I swung backwards to see if it was a junction. As we traveled in this direction, junctions would tend to splay behind us, not appear in front as the track unraveled as they had before. Swinging the Toyota around I saw that indeed, there was a track that ran roughly parallel to the one we had been on before, swinging to the east, I hoped, and Mombo.

"Giddy," I asked, interrupting his snoring, and pointed at the junction.

"Hmm," he answered, "sure," not sounding half as convinced or a fraction as concerned as I would have liked him to.

I took the turn and pushed on, driving fast again, looking forward to my pillow now more than anything else. I no longer hoped to see something rare like a pangolin or aardvark, just wanted to be home, away from people with strange relations with animals and each other.

172

The road swayed through trees, now eerie in the blue-gray light we threw, past patches of water where toads croaked and reed frogs pinged, while disappointed mosquitoes were battered by our wake.

After another hour lights appeared, sooner than I had dared hope for, and I felt a surge of relief. I pushed the throttle in again, and Gideon muttered in his sleep. Then I braked, the vehicle slewing drunkenly. Gideon flopped forward, bounced off the dash, and looked at me quizzically.

"That's not Mombo," I spoke as much to myself as to my navigator. "We're back at the baboon camp. The track must have doubled onto itself somewhere, and we didn't see it."

"I was sleeping," Gideon said, so I would know that it was my fault we were back here.

"Right," I said. It was now after midnight, and I presumed like most individuals in the bush, baboon people went to bed soon after the sun, because there was so little to do in the dark and usually no point waiting for visitors. Yet here we were again, and a flashlight beam came on, bobbing with excitement, waving us back in.

"No way," I spoke again to myself, and no matter how rude it must have seemed put the car into reverse, spun it around, and hastily shot back down the road we were covering for the fourth time.

Back we went, back into the night, Gideon making no comment on his lost opportunity for more beer or how the baboon people would perceive our ill-mannered disappearance. We passed the place we'd made our turn the last time, the tracks casting deep shadows in our lights.

A narrow moon rose, adding some light to the surrounds beyond the stars' feeble offering. Termite mounds loomed in the plains like ogres, trees twisted their roots onto the roads like adders, and fan palm leaves rattled ominously against the trunks.

We came to another junction, and without waking Gideon I took it, and noted with some relief that it struck out almost straight east. How we hadn't seen it earlier I didn't know, but surely it couldn't head back to the baboon camp, could it? If it did, I would bite the bullet and sleep wherever they put me, and as long as none tried to groom my fur it would have to do until morning.

The moon rose higher, casting more light. A termite mound with a broken façade appeared. The pockmarks on its shattered surface looked uncannily like Richard Nixon's visage, and I was thrilled. This was on the Maun road from Mombo camp, just past the duck pond. There was no way two termite mounds in Botswana could look that odd.

We hit some soft sand, right where I expected it, and I beamed, waking Giddy with my happy humming.

"Maun Road," he said flatly, then added, "Told you," and went back to sleep.

"Right you are, Giddy." I didn't care if he felt a moment of superiority and dominance, and as we swept into the back of camp, with no one to greet us, I felt a rush of endorphins, as some old biology was triggered and let me know that I was back in a place that was known to me, and safe, with friends. And while I may not be head monkey, they were my troop. Mine.

FIVE NIGHTS WITH STOMPIE

The real pulse of Mombo camp, of any camp, was always the back of the house, where day-to-day decisions were made, disasters were dealt with or disguised, and more wildlife came to visit than any tourist would imagine. Guests only saw the neat and tidy front half of the camp. They saw their tents, which marched out in a line like a propeller's blades, with the decked main area in the center as a hub. This deck held a well-stocked bar, a pool so small it would barely moisten you (and was occasionally emptied by an elephant in a few gigantic slurps), a dining table with twenty-four seats arranged around it, and a bookshelf with tomes that grew moldy every rainy season, the pages sticking together until the dry heat of September unglued them.

This was where the tourists were entertained, where they recounted the stories from their drives, where they stayed up too late to be fresh for the five a.m. start, and where they staggered dry-eyed and rough-voiced in the morning. It is where they would believe most of the camp's activity took place, but they were wrong.

Behind the deck was an administrative office, behind the office was a storeroom with water trickling over it to keep the vegetables inside cool, behind the storeroom was the kitchen, then the workshop, then the tents where the managers and guides lived.

At the very back of the camp, the two workshop attendants, Cisco and Advice, had found a place where the ground was hard packed, and each morning when the vehicles returned from safari they would hose them down over this patch, give them a rub with a gritty cloth, and park them under the shade netting next to the workshop. There the mechanic, Santos, would give them a knowing once-over. Each day they did this, the soil of the washing area became a little deeper. The hard-packed, non-mud-forming properties that made the area appealing for washing also meant that it held water, and animals learned that it was regular source for Africa's most valuable commodity. During the day there was enough activity around the camp for only the boldest baboons and some indifferent warthogs to utilize the water hole, but everything changed at night. A morning survey of tracks around its perimeter often revealed that it had been visited by lions, leopards, hyenas, and the most unwanted visitor of all, a big old Cape buffalo bull.

This buffalo made everyone's nocturnal journey to bed a risky one. His black hide blended with all but the most moonlit of nights, and if he held his head low his eyes might not reflect the beam of whatever light I carried. On many occasions after I had escorted the last guests back to their tents I would discover that they had taken the last flashlight, and I was left with the weak, nondirected glow from a kerosene lantern with which to make my way home. On a gusty night these sometimes puffed out, leaving me stranded, nervously waiting for my eyes to adjust, even more nervously noting every night sound—which would sometimes include an ominous slosh as the buffalo made his way out of the water hole, leaving me wondering if he was retreating or coming toward me.

On more than one occasion he did charge, not just me but some of the staff who weren't trained guides, and who were seriously rattled by the experience. The Botswana Wildlife Department were notified that we had a "rogue" animal, and they dispatched an officer to our camp, accompanied by two sharp-shooters from the Botswana Defence Force.

They spent three days waiting in the camp for the buffalo. Rules were made by the camp management so the tourists wouldn't see the shooting. They stated that the soldiers could only shoot while the guests were out on a drive, but the buffalo only came into camp as everyone slept in their tents, spending the day lurking deep in some thickets. On the morning the authorities were packing to leave, calling their mission a bust, I saw a buffalo step out in front of the camp, and told the manager, Chris. Moments later the wildlife officer and the army guys rocketed to the front of the camp in the back of an old Toyota, and the shooters showed that they weren't so sharp.

This buffalo had merely snorted as they approached, but broke into a tragic canter as the first shot hit him in the left hindquarter. The next was somewhere near his shoulder, and he bellowed before more shots hit him again and again throughout the body. It was an incomprehensibly brutal slaughter, and I felt like the worst kind of Judas for having given his location away. Finally, after sixteen shots, he gave one last *humph*, and died.

That night, as I walked home, a buffalo sloshed out of the water hole and galloped away. We'd either killed the wrong animal, or, as I now suspected, there were any number of buffalo using our car wash as a mud bath.

I vowed that the next time any animal was considered a threat I would do my utmost to protect it, and have no part in its demise.

It was not long after the buffalo's death that we agreed that, if anything, having the occasional buffalo at the water hole prevented some other equally dangerous animals from visiting. Hyenas in particular, already somewhat of a problem in the camp, now grew bolder, and appeared in greater numbers. They would scurry away when approached, out of range of the beam of light, but I was acutely aware that they might double back, sneak behind me, dipping their heads and licking their lips at the thought of sinking their teeth into my tasty-looking calf muscles. I would pivot regularly, and snarl at any hyena that might be there, sometimes snarling even if I couldn't see one, just in case one was outside my field of vision.

One night, after safely depositing tourists in their tents, and reassuring them as I had almost every night that no animal would claw its way through the canvas (if they did do that, I rationalized to them, we might find a different sort of accommodation), I found that once again there were no flashlights left for me. I wandered around the deck, blowing out lanterns except for the one I reserved for myself. I turned the wick higher for the widest possible circle of light and started trudging my way through the sand past the kitchen, past the workshop, and slowed as I approached the water hole by my tent, lifting the lantern high for a still wider beam.

At first I saw nothing, then noticed two glints of light. They were close to the ground. A buffalo's eyes would be higher, as they lift their head when threatened, and besides, these eyes were close together, and were forward facing. Lion.

"Bugger," I thought, and felt my insides writhe, as if they were trying to escape through my backside before they were gouged out.

Against what might seem common sense I stepped closer, not wanting to appear weak and not wanting to give the lion any opportunity to slink out of the light where I couldn't see it. There was no mane, so I immediately knew it was a female. The head was grizzled and scarred, and the body also showed marks of a life lived rough. As more of the cat became visible across the four-yard span of the water hole, I relaxed.

"Hey, Stompie," I said softly. "Where's your family?" I wasn't afraid of this lion, perhaps foolishly, but did want to know where her daughter Tippie was, and even more so her idiot grandson Dopey. Dopey wasn't threatening, but was such a goof that I could imagine him jumping on me out of curiosity and then the whole pride joining in. So I tried my utmost to keep one eye on Stompie while surveying for the other pride members.

There was no sign of them, and Stompie was not showing interest in me so I backed to my tent, swiveling periodically until I made it into my room. My adrenaline was high, which made it impossible to get to sleep so I listened to the repeated *purrrp* of a scops owl, the faraway sound of an elephant breaking branches, and the snuffling of a porcupine that might just get itself eaten if it went for a drink. I heard no scuffle, though, and finally drifted off. The next morning Stompie was not outside my room, and her tracks meandered into the rain-tree forest behind the managers' tents. This was not unusual behavior, and I imagined that she had been left behind by the pride and was now trying to keep up.

Stompie's pride was the first set of lions I had seen in Botswana, and they impressed me immediately with their strangeness. Chris had driven me up to them with what I thought was alarming speed, but they hadn't flinched, not even when he parked within inches of one of the few tail tips visible. The only reaction was from a young male who gave the leonine approximation of a smile and sniffed at our tire before chasing his tail and flopping back down. I'd never seen a lion chase its tail before, but his delight may have been because it was intact. His mother, Tippie, who led the pride, was missing the tip of her tail. "Hyena bit it off when she was young," Chris explained.

Even though she wasn't the oldest lion in the group, Tippie was the pride's leader. The eldest lion, which Chris thought was about thirteen years old, had an even briefer appendage. Only half a foot long, it still flicked irritably at the flies that surrounded her battle-scared, chipped-tooth visage. This was Stompie, Chris said, a name derived from a South African term for a cigarette butt. The tawny stump protruding from her rear end did indeed resemble a discarded stub. Strangest of all, though, was Stompie's inclusion in this family. Lions are unsentimental beasts, and an individual as aged and incapable of hunting as Stompie was should have been left behind long ago.

It appeared she may finally have been discarded, for the next night, this time armed with a flashlight, I encountered her again. She was on the move, well ahead of me, making her way to the water hole. I knew our paths would bisect, but I felt no apprehension. I just stopped, and watched as she came to the water. She knelt to drink, with a defined care that suggested her knees pained her, and gave quick, noisy slurps. As I angled around her she paused, glanced my way, and held my gaze for a few moments. It remains the only time in my life that I have stood only yards from a wild lion, with nothing to protect me, and felt no fear.

She went back to her drinking, still keeping an eye on me, and I sidled to my doorway, a simple slab of timber in a plain frame, surrounded by nothing but canvas. From the doorway I watched Stompie finish her drink, then settle lower onto her haunches before flopping onto her side, in a position familiar to anyone who has ever owned a house cat.

She breathed quickly, often a sign that a cat is digesting, but her ribs showed through and I knew that she was just exhausted, and maybe ill. "Goodnight, Stompie," I called as I shut my door, "hope you make it through the night."

She did. In the morning I caught her walking again, but even slower, and she settled within sight of our tents. Chris, Grant, and I spread the word amongst the staff to be careful around the management and guides' quarters. Nobody mentioned the wildlife department, but we all knew one thing. Lions don't normally attack people, unless they are defending their cubs, or unless they are old and unable to hunt anything faster and stronger than our feeble species. If she stayed in the camp, we had an unavoidable problem.

The next night she was at the water hole again, and by now I looked forward to seeing her there. There certainly hadn't been any buffalo hanging around now that she was here, even though in her condition she had no chance of catching one, and would have been as easy to trample as a baby.

Lions called from the near distance that night, and I listened to hear if Stompie would call back. She would know the voices of her family, and reply if it was them. She stayed silent, though, and I wondered if it was another pride or if she was now so weakened that she couldn't even call. If that was the case, she might not even make the morning.

In the middle of the night, which wasn't too long after I had fallen asleep, something woke me. This was no easy feat. In Japan I once slept through a sizable earthquake, and in Africa had become inured to the calls of animals, and usually nothing short of fireworks would wake me until my alarm rang.

I sat up, figuring out what noises were relics from the dream I'd been having. My tent was dark, the only light coming through a hole in the roof. I heard a giggle outside.

It was a sinister sound. An evil yipping followed it, then a whoop. The hyenas were excited about something. They burst into the screeches that always made my skin prickle and nerves in my teeth flare. It sounded like a woman being attacked.

They must be going after Stompie. Maybe they'd watched her from a distance for a while, maybe each night that she'd been there, waiting for her weakness to reach the point that they could move in and administer the coup de grâce. It was awful to imagine what must be happening to her. The hyenas wouldn't take her face on, but some would distract her from the front while others circled behind, nipping at her hindquarters, slowly bleeding her until she died. I wanted to go out and help her, but knew it was likely that the hyenas in their excited state would turn on me and pull me to pieces before I could help. Stompie herself could misinterpret my aims and go for the softest target in defending herself, which would certainly be the weakling human.

And I was afraid. I considered Stompie, like many of the animals at Mombo, a friend, even though she would never reciprocate the sentiment. I also believed that I would help any friend in trouble, but now just lay in my tent listening to her being killed, cursing my cowardice, and not sleeping until moments before my alarm went off.

In the gray light I crept from my room. I expected to find her carcass in the water hole or beside it, but there was no body. There were hyena tracks in every direction, some paused, some digging in, telling a story of patient waiting followed by short darts of speed. The water hole itself had no definable edge, and liquid had splashed and splattered all around it. I circled it, and saw the occasional lion pugmark, but no clear trail of where Stompie had gone.

Had she made it through the night, only to walk off to die? What kind of fight had she put up? Had the hyenas killed her outright and dragged her body away? That would have left a flattened patch in the grass, but there was none. I scanned the ground further, but needed to get to work so gave up after a few minutes, and fired up my Land Rover.

On my drive that morning I found Tippie, her sister, the three cubs, and Dopey. They had just killed a warthog, small meat for a family that size. Dopey was far too old to still be with his mother, but our dominant males in the north had been recently driven out, and with no one to replace them Dopey kept living at home. So excited was he by their kill that he decided to climb a palm tree. Halfway up he realized how much he weighed, how great was the drop, and his inability to turn around. With a great howl followed by a dust-disturbing splat, he crashed to the ground. It was the silliest thing I'd seen a lion do, but my amusement was tempered by their location. The pride was a long way from camp. A long way from Stompie. If she wasn't already dead, to survive she'd need the pride to come to camp and make a kill right under her nose.

That night I made sure I had a flashlight. My vehicle was parked not in its bay, but outside my room, ready to ride forth and defend a distressed lion if needed. I read in my room for a while, periodically walking to my open door and shining into the night, seeing no sign of Stompie. When she did arrive it was no surprise that I didn't hear her, but it was unnerving that she was right outside my tent. She had her back to me, and didn't flick an ear at the light playing over her angular hips and the recent cuts and slashes from hyena teeth on her back. Maybe her phantom tail tip did curl, but the rest of her stayed still, resting for the few meters she had to walk to the water.

Many people in Africa have sated hunger temporarily by filling up with water, and I wondered if Stompie might be doing the same. I also wondered at the pain her empty belly must be causing her. She finally stood, staggered the last few steps, a pitiful sight, and flopped again by the water hole.

The next morning she hadn't moved, and didn't pay me any attention when I drove past her. As the sun rose she shuffled into shade, but was still within the bounds of the camp, opening her eyes occasionally to watch the staff as they did their daily duties, breathing shallowly, looking desperate, hungry, and maybe, just maybe now there was real danger in her presence. Nothing is slower than a human, nothing weaker, nothing has such blunt teeth and claws. We are the easiest meal in the bush, the least-fast food, and if it wasn't for our ancestors striking fear into all species with their use of weapons, there might be far fewer of us.

"Can't we just give her some meat?" the catering manager asked. "Not filet, of course, that's too bloody difficult to get, but bacon, chops, something?"

Grant, Chris, and myself all shook our heads in unison, knowing that it would only train Stompie to think of humans as a source of food. It was a mistake made by many people over many years with many species, and it always ended badly.

I didn't see her the next night, even though I waited as late as I could before exhaustion claimed me. Just before dawn I heard her. She'd crept back in. *How-um*, she moaned, a contact call given by lions that have lost their pride. She called her family again, *How-um*. It is a mournful sound at the best of times, but now it pained me to hear it. No answer came, and she was gone by the time I slapped my alarm clock, pulled on my shirt, shorts, and sandals, and left my room.

The next night she didn't come, and no tracks were around the water hole.

The night after, I approached the water hole with some enthusiasm, sure that I would find her there. I was walking briskly and thrilled as the light picked up a gleam. The reflected eye moved at my approach, raised up, too high for a lion.

"Bugger," I thought, and backed into a thorn bush as the buffalo charged off, trailing mud and indignation.

Nothing the next night. Or from then on. I saw Nicky the leopard at our water hole soon after, baboons during the day, furtively flicking their brows at the workshop guys who occasionally threw sticks at them, warthogs came every day, buffalo at night, hyenas, an elephant that loomed from the darkness like a dinosaur come to life, but never Stompie. Never again did she come to the water hole in the back of Mombo Camp.

"Waaaaa! All mobiles, I've got *tau*." It was Nandi, a guide who had recently joined the camp letting us know he had found lions. He started every sentence with the exclamation "Waaaaa!" for no reason that I ever figured out. "They're by Honeymoon Pan, slowly mobile north." We had a pattern for calling in sightings. Guides announced what animal they'd found, spoken in Setswana so the tourists wouldn't understand where they were and what the animals were doing.

"How many you got?" I asked, wondering which pride it was.

"Three *basadi*, one *moena*, three *manyani*." Three females, one male, and three young.

It wasn't a giveaway as to what pride it was, but I was nearby so I went to look for myself. It was Tippie's pride, and in the time it took me to get there they had brought down a kudu, an unusual kill for them to make in daylight. Dopey was snarling at the rest, even with a mouthful of meat. The only time he ever looked serious was when food was involved. Tippie was also there, as was her younger sister. The unnamed sister had three young, and these clambered over the top of their family, scrapping for the meat they would need to survive. Lions give nothing away without a fight, and young lions often starve, but this was a large antelope and would easily feed them all.

They had made the kill right beside one of our tracks, a sweeping curve of road that followed a tree line. Nandi pointed to a feverberry tree, indicating there was one more lion there. The bush rustled, and the animal emerged. I couldn't believe my eyes. "Stompie!" I called out, no doubt confusing the tourists to whom I had just painstakingly explained the names Tippie and Dopey. She'd found her family, who knew how or when, and while still thin, she was moving far better than when I'd last seen her three weeks earlier.

With a wheeze she squeezed her way between her daughters, who both gave a deep rumble at her intrusion. "Give an old girl a break!" I thought, but knew that lions had no such niceties. She sank her teeth into the meat and I could almost taste it myself, taste the life she was getting from the one just taken.

Hyenas arrived at the kill that afternoon, bold in the region since the big male lions had left. But Dopey was an impressive-looking animal now, even if his intellect and instincts remained dubious. With a roar and some ill-timed but purposeful swipes of his paw he kept the hyenas at bay, and the pride grew fat over two days of feeding.

This area had always been the core territory of Tippie's pride, but they were an aging pride, with only one breeding female, who was having to rebuff the increased advances of her idiot nephew while hoping for some real males to appear. They were also being pressured by a new pride to the region, called the Matata Pride, far stronger in numbers and youth.

Eventually they just left. Nobody can say where they went, or if some remnant of their pride exists on some other island in the Okavango, perhaps known by a new name, maybe rebuilding in strength. Dopey would have been driven out by stronger males, but by some miracle may have acquired a territory of his own for a while.

My head tells me that by now Stompie is long dead, Tippie too. Even the youngest female would need a miracle to still be roaming the Delta, as lions live a short life in the wild. Dopey, no matter his strength, would now be too old to survive. My heart tells me, though, that the pride still lives on somewhere. They are, if nothing else, descended from a great survivor.

Voyages in the Coffin

"Advice!" I was shouting, screaming even. I had just been on the receiving end of a thorough telling-off by Grant, who had recently taken over the management of Mombo. "I need Advice!" I shouted again, then, "Surprise!" Shouting "Surprise!" in our camp could mean one of two things. It meant either "Surprise!" as in "There's a snake in your bed!" or that you were summoning one of the ladies who worked in the laundry. I suspect her parents hadn't planned her.

"Yes?" Surprise answered carefully, perhaps noting the white spittle at the corner of my mouth.

"I need Advice," I said again. "Have you seen him?" I had recently been promoted to assistant manager of Mombo camp, and Advice was my assistant. I wasn't really meant to have an assistant, and officially his job title was something more like workshop attendant. I enjoyed his company, though, so usually picked him whenever I needed someone to work with on the regular maintenance issues that plagued our aging camp.

Advice appeared from the workshop, wiping his small hands on a greasy cloth that only made them dirtier, and beamed at me. His smile was so disarming that it was hard to be angry, but we had a big problem in camp and I suspected him to be the cause.

"*Yebo?*" he said, still smiling.

"Last week, when I asked you to measure the fuel, you said that we had 3,200 liters of diesel, right?"

"*Yebo,*" he said again, maintaining the smile, still rubbing at a spot on his hand that was only getting more smeared.

"Come with me, please," I said, my voice taut, and marched to the two large tanks we used to store fuel. "Which stick did you use?" I asked.

"The one that we use," Advice said, still with his disarming smile.

The one that we used, and always had, was notched at regular intervals along its length so with a simple dip into the tank a reasonably accurate assessment of our fuel supply could be given.

The stick had been broken in half.

"Advice, you didn't think that because the stick is broken you might have to give a different number?"

"Eh eh," he said (meaning "no"), "that stick, it is always right. It is a very clever stick."

"Right," I said.

We had a problem.

Mombo was one of the most expensive camps in Botswana to visit, but it was in a rather decrepit state. The safari company was able to maintain such a high price because the game viewing was jaw-droppingly good. The ten-year lease would be up in a year's time, and the camp wasn't going to be rebuilt until the company was sure they had resecured the location from the Botswana Government for the next term. Now we had almost run out of diesel for our vehicles, and it might be several days before a truck could get to us with emergency supplies. The small planes we used were by law not allowed to carry fuel to us, a policy strictly monitored and enforced by the government. Grant had explained all this to me after he dressed me down for not checking the fuel myself.

It wasn't declared a punishment, or a demotion, but I was given tourists to guide, and everybody's least-favorite vehicle to do it in. The Coffin.

At one point the company had decided against buying a vehicle from a regular supplier, and acquired this monstrosity. Like the rest of our game drive vehicles, it was a Land Rover, but any resemblance to a road vehicle stopped past the hood. The windscreen was absent, the roof chopped off. In most vehicles the tourists sat on tiered seats behind the driver in a frame the same width as the wheelbase. The Coffin, though, had an enormous polyhedral tub welded onto its frame, into which were bolted three rows of seats with an aisle between them as if a hostess would appear at some point on the drive to serve drinks. Entry to the Coffin was from the rear, accessed by a drop-down gate like something you'd use to herd cattle onto a truck.

The structure on the back was enormously heavy, and the car had no power steering, so driving the Coffin was like pushing an unwilling warthog through mud. Its level seats meant most people had a view of the heads of those in front, but they were in dire need of a better vantage as the Coffin's girth meant normally distant thorn branches whipped hungrily at the tourists from beside the tracks.

But it was our only fully fueled vehicle at this moment, and short of telling people we could walk to look for animals instead, it was the best option for me to take my drive in. I approached the vehicle with trepidation, checked that all tires were inflated, and that it had a spare wheel, jack, and spanner. I made sure that the fan belt was tight, and that the oil was at its required level. Normally I'd have stopped my inspection at the tires, but this was the Coffin. I believed it was cursed.

Being superstitious goes against my scientific mind-set, so black cats can cross my path all day without me frowning, mirrors are just any number of things I have broken that I blame on clumsiness as opposed to bad luck, and the number 13 holds no fear. I don't walk under ladders, though, not because it is bad luck, but because it's a stupid thing to do.

My belief in the bad luck of the Coffin came after a succession of drives in it where I saw no predators. This happens occasionally on safari, and while it rudely discounts the many animals that are observed such as zebras, giraffes, and impalas and other antelopes, it is deeply stressful for the guide who knows that tourists are in Africa to see animals that kill things. Every time I took the Coffin out the lions hid, the leopards found the deepest bush to go into, cheetahs became extinct, and wild dogs were as mythic as unicorns. There are only so many things you can say about acacia trees before discontented grumbling comes from the back seat.

Yet my dislike for the Coffin wasn't based purely upon its ability to render wildlife invisible. I knew it wanted to kill me.

This theory was based on rigorous scientific methodology. The Coffin had been at Mombo well before me, and had seen me destroy some of its brethren (two cars I drowned, one I impaled on a tree stump while following wild dogs). Maybe it was revenge it plotted, maybe it just didn't like me, but I was convinced that one of us would have to leave Mombo soon. This was solidified by an incident a few months earlier when I'd had a rare day off from guiding, with only one duty in the afternoon. A pilot was bringing some freight in, and would then stay overnight. As soon as I had him and the food he'd brought back in camp, we could go on a staff drive.

As exhausting as it could be taking out tourists day after day, I still aimed to spend as many waking moments as possible in the bush, watching animals, so was moving faster than normal soon after hearing the plane buzz the camp, ahead of schedule.

"Kevin!" I shouted to a friend from another camp who was also spending a night at Mombo. "Come and give me a hand with freight."

Normally Kevin had a quick and sarcastic answer to anything I said, often sprinkled with all the profanities he couldn't use in front of tourists, but this time he quietly acquiesced. The only vehicle available to us was the Coffin, and we jumped into the front seat and roared from the back of the camp, past the baobab tree where church services were held by our staff on Sunday nights, kicked dust out of the sharp bend before the track went through some thick acacia scrub, and pushed through some deep divots that held water in the rainy season and became home to myriad bullfrogs that I'd taken great pains to avoid squashing. Now I had no such impediments, and was driving fast. The speedometer didn't work, so I had no idea of my real speed, this gauge book-ended by a dead fuel indicator and inoperative temperature gauge.

We burst from the scrub with about thirty yards of open ground before we reached the plane, now sitting idle as the pilot, named Sven, tied it down.

I had a habit that I'd picked up on game drives, of switching off the engine and letting the vehicle glide to a rest. It saved a very small amount of fuel and allowed the last few yards of approach to the animals to be nearly silent.

What I had not considered on this approach was that like so many things on this vehicle, the brakes did not work. As my foot pumped madly at the pedal, we kept moving at a speed that would result in a very loud bang when we hit something. Since we were aimed at an airplane, and as they are quite expensive,

I turned the wheel so we would collide with something cheaper, like a tree.

With the turn, I finally found something on the Coffin that worked. At the smallest rotation, the steering lock clicked on and the wheel stopped dead. Kevin looked at me quizzically, quite reasonably wondering why I was maintaining a collision course with the plane. "Brakes don't work," I explained. "Steering lock does."

"Oh," was all he replied, and with what I thought was admirable calm he put himself in the brace position against the dashboard. I kept pumping wildly at the brakes, but the pedal stayed soft, the wheel stiff.

Sven was on the far side of the plane so had no idea of the danger he was in.

I was ready to shout a warning when I had an idea. My foot came off the brake, and planted hard on the clutch. I threw the stick into first gear.

I lifted my foot from the clutch.

Gears meshed, then chewed at each other, a god-awful sound of metal tearing at metal, followed by a costly-sounding *Clank! Clank! Clank!* Kevin and I were thrown forward, then back, then forward as the Coffin bucked against its momentum on locking wheels. The plane drew closer, but we were slowing.

Our angle would have had us hit right by the mercifully still propeller. Most times this came to rest with one blade up, two angled down, like the symbol on a Mercedes, but Sven on this day had managed to have two blades facing up, the third straight down. The snout of the Coffin came to a grinding rest within an inch of the lower blade, an upper one angled over the bonnet.

"Good thinking," Kevin said, still calm. "That would have been a crap way to die."

Despite the chunks of gearbox that littered the track behind us, the Coffin was unfortunately repairable, and far less costly to replace than a propeller would have been. Somehow I wasn't even reprimanded for damaging yet another vehicle.

But I had had too many bad experiences in the Coffin to be happy about my upcoming drive. Grant warned me not to go too far on my safari and to stop often, as we needed to preserve every drop of diesel we had, and the fluttering began in my stomach. This would not be a good drive, I was sure.

It wasn't. The animals, as I had feared, were in hiding. We did see impalas, but they were as common as traffic is in a city, and though they are very pretty, their appeal soon wears off. I stopped for them all, though, on the pretense that a leopard might be stalking them. It was rubbish, and I suspect some of the tourists were figuring it out.

"We came for leopards, not deer!" a German barked at me.

"Antelopes," I softly corrected him.

Suddenly one of the impalas gave a snort, kicked its back legs out, and the entire herd took off, flinging their front legs high and pumping their back legs, a rocking and rolling run that they reserved for occasions when Africa's greatest hunting animal was pursuing them.

"Dogs!" I shouted.

"Where?" one of the tourists asked, quite reasonably.

"Don't know!" I answered. I couldn't see them and had a moment of doubt. The impalas' panic and dash into thick vegetation was not how they would react to a leopard. If they'd spotted a lion or cheetah they would snort, move out of its way, but hang around to watch it so it couldn't sneak up on them. They were gone, though, indicating they knew the predators coming after them were distance runners, prepared to chase them until they were caught. But where were they? Had the Coffin's curse struck again and the dogs vanished in puffs of dust?

Then they surrounded us, a blur of tan, black, and white, swept past, and sped into the bush.

"Hang on!" I shouted, hauled on the heavy wheel, and shot after them. The dogs move at such speed, through whatever terrain the chase demands, that there is no time to plot and plan which way to turn. They are just smaller than the German shepherds that they share their coloring with, and so they are able to squeeze through tight gaps that a Land Rover can not. Every time I was with the dogs my aim was to see them bring their prey down, and so far I had never achieved it, always arriving as they were finishing up the meat before a larger predator arrived and stole it.

With my right foot planted, we pursued the chase. A hornbill bursting from a bush ahead indicated where they had gone, and I angled us in that direction. The strip of vegetation we were in was narrow and from it we came to a grassy plain, just in time to see a trailing dog dash through a shallow channel on its far side before heading into a copse of trees, its general direction bearing for our camp.

The Coffin may not have had a top speed that would impress fans of motor racing, but with no roof and a high seating position, it felt like flight. Despite a reputation for poor driving skills in general, at high speeds, with no time for thought to get in the way, my driving became instinctive—I'd swerve around burrows, hit only bushes that would spring straight back up, dab at the breaks for a turn before remembering they didn't work and slide the car instead, and, my favorite trick, pass through impossibly narrow gaps. It is the closest I have ever come to feeling graceful.

This close to camp I was familiar with not just the tracks but the bush in between, and knew that two large trees had a gap between them that by all appearances was too narrow to take a Land Rover. But I knew from experience that if you hit the gap at an angle, and halfway through shimmied the wheel, you could wiggle through. This was the gap I needed to dissect if I was to keep up with the dogs. Maybe my luck had just turned in this car. We'd found predators, now I was sure we'd see the action the tourists craved. Whoops of delight from the back let me know that my driving was appreciated, and spurred a dump of logic-devouring testosterone through my system. The gap approached, the tourists saw I was going for it, and their whoops turned to gasps. "Surely he can't be aiming for that?" they must have been thinking, just like every other tourist had before I dazzled them with the shimmy. As I angled the bonnet just right, the testosterone eased, by the merest fraction, and a salient fact came to me. The Coffin wasn't the same as our other vehicles that scraped through this gap by a cat's whisker. It was significantly wider.

The brakes did nothing but squeak as I slammed my foot down, pain flaring in my knee. This was subsumed by the pain in my abdomen as we came to a violent halt. I had slid forward in the seat, and the lower half of the wheel collected my lowest ribs, punching the air from my lungs and whipping my forehead forward to fold me over double.

A tourist toppled clear out of the tub, landing on me from behind. A largish woman, she later told me that she was grateful for the cushioning I had provided. "Part of the job," I said while politely smiling, even though my face still smarted from the steering wheel logo embedded in it when she landed on me.

Remarkably, nobody was hurt apart from me, even though all had been vaulted forward a full row of seats. The Coffin's rear wheels were frozen in the air, the front forced into the soil and leaf litter.

By the time we had been towed out, other vehicles had seen the rampaging dogs make two kills, feed their pups, and settle in for the day. They saw lions too, but I didn't have the time or diesel to drive to the place they had been sighted.

We limped home, and the rarely sober mechanic took a look at the barely dented panels where we had been pegged.

"Tough stuff," he said, banging appreciatively at the machine's flanks. As he drove it toward the workshop, though, there was a resounding crash and the entire tub fell off the chassis. The whole thing crumpled like cardboard, only one small weld having held it in place for our drive back to camp.

I had killed the Coffin.

"Not good," I was told, when asked about my prospects for having that afternoon off from guiding, as I had quite a headache.

"Okay," I said resignedly, "any chance I can have a different car?"

TWELVE PACES

My concentration lapsed at the sight of the baobabs. They were unexpected, appearing in a landscape that up to now had been dominated by feral orange groves and coastal vegetation, punctuated by the occasional village, or a random traveler walking down the middle of the tar road on which I'd been driving the last few hours. So I pulled over to the side of the road, something I had been specifically told not to do, and started running to the trees and the delicious fruit they bore before a thought struck me.

Why, here in impoverished Mozambique, would the fruit still be on the tree? Why hadn't the locals taken them for their own consumption? The answer was now obvious, and I stopped suddenly, jarring my bad right knee and balancing on one foot.

I was standing in a minefield.

This country's civil war had been over for more than two years, but munitions still littered the country. More than two million land mines were estimated to be spread around the nation, but even the experts that this information came from said that the figure was a very rough guess. I'd been staying in Maputo with my friend Chris, and it was his car that I was driving. To repay his generosity for lending me the vehicle while I was on my leave and enjoying Mozambique's coast, I'd already driven it into a pole, denting the door quite severely. Now it seemed he might not get it back at all, as I stood rooted to the spot, imagining I'd never muster the bravery to move my feet again.

The trees in front of me were closer than the car, and I couldn't help but covet the eggplant-sized fruit hanging from the branches. Globular and coated in a fine fur, these were not juicy like an orange, but powdery on the inside, with seeds the size of coffee beans. The powdery coating was tart, and I'd planned on mixing it with water and sugar to make a sort of lemonade that was incredibly refreshing on a hot day. If I'd kept running another three or four paces I might have made it to the trees, and after knocking down a few fruit would have walked around them collecting my bounty, before strolling back using shorter paces, arms full. The thought of how many extra paces I almost took made me burst into a sweat. Was I experiencing what it was like as an animal on this continent? You were looking for food, then *boom!* (or *snarl, roar,* or whatever noise the creature biting you made) and it was all over. Then it hit me, surprisingly for the first time, that it wasn't just animals that faced this scenario each day, but many of the people in Africa as well. Now I was one step away from joining them.

My reverie was snapped by voices behind me. I pivoted on the spot, one hundred and eighty degrees, until I was facing Chris's car again, which seemed a cursedly long way away. A small crowd had appeared, and I marveled at this phenomenon. No matter how remote the part of Africa you are in, no matter how long you have driven without seeing a soul, once you stop a car people arrive, as if the earth has sprouted them. Many times they have something to sell you, food types ranging from fresh roasted corn to exotic tasties like mouse kebabs—furry rodents, teeth in a grimace, impaled on a skewer. Even my adventurous palate had always refused this offering, though the grilled locusts weren't bad. I couldn't believe my eyes, but a small market was forming as the locals gathered to watch the crazy white guy who was standing on one leg in the minefield. Even as they milled and swirled, not one of them stepped off the safety of the tar.

I scanned the expectant faces in the crowd, hoping for someone with a look that would convey a way out of here, perhaps holding up a quick scribble of mine locations and where I should step next. Some of the women did have unveiled sympathy on their faces. I didn't like the idea of pity—pity suggested they didn't think I'd get out. One man's face stuck out. He was smiling at me, true glee at my predicament writ large on his features. As my eyes met his, he splayed his hands in a motion suggesting fireworks and, showing that some words are universal, mouthed "*boom.*" My heart sank at this, and my knee buckled.

I caught myself close to the ground, wavered, and fell forward. I let a sound like a sob out as my hand hit dirt, but I didn't hear a click. The crowd gasped. My heart raced, my mouth filled with spit, and I wanted the bathroom more than ever in my life. Chris had explained to me that most of the mines in Mozambique were Czech made, mainly plastic and therefore hard to locate with metal detectors. A step would depress a trigger, and as the foot lifted the mine would pop out of the ground to groin height, then blow. They were designed to maim, not kill, as it took up more personnel. The victim would have to be carried by two able-bodied people from where they lay, and if they lived would be unable to do much of the hard work that survival in Africa depends upon.

My hand still on the ground, my foot still planted, I cursed my stupidity. The bloody oranges growing by the road hadn't been eaten, and that was a giveaway that I was in a mine zone. The people I'd passed walking on the road, not beside it, were another sure sign that there were mines around.

Stupid, stupid, stupid, I shouted inside my head, and pushed up with my hand, then leaped forward, knowing my knee might give way again. There was only one safe way out, and that was to put my feet exactly where they had landed as I ran in. I may have missed mines by yards, or by mere inches. I've never been a particularly good tracker, but as I was propelled forward I clearly saw the indents my feet had made as I ran to the trees.

In the air I realized I'd jumped too hard, and would overshoot. With another sob I landed, my voice masking any click a trigger may have made. The crowd, now numbering around twenty, gave a small cheer that I had landed safely. I scanned the ground ahead, but this was short grass, and didn't show tracks well. A patch of paler blades might be where my foot had previously landed, and therefore would be safe. I cursed the length of my running stride, as it seemed a long way to jump with any accuracy, particularly with only one foot as a launching pad. Then I remembered the track behind me that I had overshot, and craning my neck placed my right foot onto it, closing my eyes and savoring for a moment the luxury of having both feet on the ground. I gauged the distance back to the car, figuring that it was ten paces. I'd made only two back, and already my legs were wobbly, my strength wavering, my bowels unsure whether or not to evacuate on the spot.

My nostrils flared as I drew breath, in and out, scanning for the place I must aim for. Again it was in grass, but ahead was a sandy patch where my tracks should be easy to see. I leaped at a trampled area and this time landed dead-on. My senses had never felt so sharp, the smell of grass and dust strong on the air, my hearing acute enough to detect the crumpling of grass underfoot. I drew some confidence from this, further boosted by my clear boot marks in front of me. My countdown continued as I easily leaped through paces nine, eight, and seven, the crowd whooping at my speed, perhaps thinking I was making a desperate and blind dash. They hollered, some in support, some in derision as I poised on a single leg again, looking balefully at the grass that was growing almost the whole way back to the verge. The edge of this patch was slightly higher grass, and my sharpened eyesight could see some blades that had been roughly shoved aside, so I landed square on those, wobbled a little, teetered, and regathered balance. "Heh heh," I chuckled with some relief, and the crowd found this uproariously funny. Even Boomman applauded me now.

There was a problem, though. The grass in front of me was uniform. No bent blades, no paler undersides showing, nothing to show where the remaining five steps were.

I felt that now I had a feeling for the length of my stride, and where I should land. I made a leap of faith, and launched, my right leg with the weak knee coming down.

Even over the increasingly loud onlookers the click was audible.

"Aaaaaaaaaaaaaah," I let out an involuntary sound, a noise I'd heard someone make once as they were being electrocuted, a desperate, bestial call.

"Oooh," the crowd said in unison. They couldn't have heard the click but had read the despair in my voice. The support I'd felt growing for me vanished, and a woman carrying a basket of oranges on her back began to cry. Tears welled in my eyes and my chest heaved. I'd rather die than be maimed here, I thought. Let it be quick, I thought. Just let it be quick, and I looked down.

Twig. There was a twig under my boot. A bloody, bastard twig, snapped in half. I laughed at it, a strangled gurgle of a laugh but a laugh nonetheless, and the woman cried harder, mistaking my sound for terror. Maybe she had a son my age lost in the war, I imagined, or maybe she was just a sensitive soul. The people of this country had faced more than twenty years of brutal warfare, so I didn't resent the few that were taking delight in my predicament. After all, it was not long ago that my culture fed people to lions for entertainment.

I jumped from the twig, blind again to where I must land, aware that if I was off on my last jump I'd double the discrepancy this time. Four. I landed. No click. Three paces to go. The last two footprints I needed to land in were visible from where I stood, after which I'd be in the safety of the vehicle.

The problem was my next step. I couldn't see where it should be, and standing on one leg for so long, so many times, had made me extremely fatigued. I wiped my forearm across my brow and flicked away the sweat. Someone in the crowd shouted something to me, maybe encouragement, maybe a warning, and I leaped again.

My foot hit the grass and skidded. I'd taken a long leap to match my loping stride. My foot slid forward and I started to fall. Instincts kicked in and to avoid tearing my groin, my back leg came down, the toe digging hard into the ground, my knee also connecting with the earth. I was in the first stages of the splits, my momentum still pushing me forward but my physiology not allowing any further movement. Instead my torso wrenched and I tipped sideways, flinging a hand out to catch myself.

My fingers splayed and hit grass, I wobbled, then held firm. My audience had gone quiet but now erupted into shouts. I didn't speak their language. Some of it would have been their local tongue; some shouts directed at me were in Portuguese, but I know little in that language beyond terms for seafood and booze.

Had they heard a click? Some definitely thought so, because they had backed away from the blast they expected. Others argued against them, arms waving, fingers wagging, declaring me safe. Boom-man appeared to be taking bets. I wondered what my odds were. Life was cheap in Africa, something I'd known a long while, yet I couldn't help resent the joy he was taking from my predicament.

I moved tentatively. Pushing up with my fingers, I was in a sprinter's stretch, the foot out front with toes raised, the back leg in contact with the ground in two places. If I had depressed a mine, my height was low enough that it would pop to face height before blowing. Yet I rose from my stance, fatalistically, and used my momentum to jump to my next track, my muscles tense throughout my body, my jaw aching from the clench I'd held it in. No explosion. One more step, and I was at the car.

It was a simple thing to do, a shorter pace because I hadn't broken into a run when I first stepped out. A simple thing that seemed incredibly difficult. The tension of the eleven paces I'd made had released, too soon, and that last little step looked like a chasm to me, one that would surely swallow me whole. Tears spattered my boots, surprising me, but not as much as the woman who'd been crying earlier now shouting at me, indecipherable words but the meaning clear—"move your backside, get out of there, one more step."

I took it, and clung to the side of the vehicle. The woman offered me an orange, then asked for some metical, the local currency. I paid her, waved away all the other vendors as I couldn't imagine eating ever again, and got behind the seat.

I sat there shaking for a few minutes, then started the engine. Looking over my left shoulder I gazed at the baobabs, their gray, elephant skin bark imposing.

So close, I thought, so close, and drove on.

HUNTED

All I wanted was to get to bed. But the lion would not move, and I could not get past her.

Only a few minutes earlier I had been making my way along the wooden walkway that linked the luxury tents of Mombo Camp. A scops owl gave its *prrrping* call nearby, and somewhere above me leaves rustled—perhaps a monkey restless in sleep, or a genet pursuing desperate prey.

As I passed the last tent, the walkway I was on sloped steeply down from head height until it reached the ground. It ran at ankle height for a few yards before sloping steeply up again, until it reached a height where you could walk safely without threat from predators. This dip to ground level was not just for late-night thrills, but served two practical functions. It separated the newly rebuilt, sixteen-bed main camp of Mombo from the smaller, eight-bed Little Mombo, while also providing a place for giraffes and elephants to cross through the camp should they want to. All other animals could pass underneath the high walkways, and I scanned the ground as I went, wondering if any interesting nocturnal creatures were out and about.

I was no longer based at Mombo, as I had taken a position as guide trainer for the company, only occasionally leading trips for tourists. I was taking a group through four different camps, and had been up at five every morning for two weeks, but was still thrilled to be back in my favorite camp and old home.

The beam of my flashlight first caught the lioness as she emerged from some shrubs and walked to the crossing. She glanced at me, but didn't seem concerned by my presence, at least not then. I didn't recognize her, in part because it was night and also because she was not accompanied by her pride members. She padded purposefully toward the timber slats that sat only ankle height off the dust, and placed a paw onto the walkway. Then she withdrew it. Her nose wrinkled, and she gingerly stretched her paw out again. The entire walkway had been oiled not long before, and she clearly found the slimy sensation underfoot disturbing. She put her left paw in again, and took her left paw out, and I started humming "do the hokey-pokey" to myself.

I enjoyed the comedy of her indecision for a while, and liked seeing such a hunter unable to face the challenge of a two-foot crossing. I also admired her determination to beat the challenge rather than moving to her left or right a few yards and crossing underneath, like I had seen plenty of other lions, hyenas, and leopards do. Instead she hunkered down, and faced the offending boards, pondering her problem.

Just how tired I was settled in within seconds, and all amusement started to fade. Part of my job was to be the last of the group to bed. It was now late, the tent I was using was only a hundred paces from me, and this stubborn cat was blocking my way.

Nighttime in Africa belongs to predators, and only a fool walks in the bush after dark. But I figured that since I was still up high I would look far bigger than the reality. So I took a step toward the lioness, shining the light at her eyes, and hoarsely whispered, "Bugger off!" as loudly as I could without waking the guests in the tents behind me.

She didn't bugger off, nor was she threatened by my height advantage. Instead, she fluidly shifted her body so she was facing me, hunched herself lower, flattened her ears, and set her expression. If I had seen her like this on a drive I would have

excitedly explained, "That's a stalking face—she's seen something to eat!"

Oops, I thought, keeping the flashlight aimed at her eyes
and wondering how fresh the batteries were. I was sure that she
would look away from the beam, and when her focus was broken
I would back up a bit. But she kept staring, *through* the light, at
me. Her intensity spoke of nothing but a devotion to eating me.

I took a step back, and she rose with quicksilver elegance,
pausing halfway from her crouch, a motion I had seen and
admired so many times while watching cats hunt. Now I found
it more than a little disturbing. Behind me, I knew, was a guest
tent, and opposite it a canvas structure where curios were sold
during the day. But how many paces they were away I couldn't
recall, and there was no way I was taking my eyes off the lion.

Neither of us moved for a while; then she slowly, slowly
settled back onto her haunches, her head staying steady the
whole time. I took a step back and she stayed down, so I backed
up again, lifting my sandaled feet to an exaggerated height to
ensure I wouldn't trip and expose my rump to her nondiscerning
palate. My hand trailed over the rough logs of the handrails as
I went, and a splinter that felt as big as a tree jabbed me in the
palm.

"Bastard!" I hissed, maybe loud enough to wake the guests,
a cardinal sin at such an expensive camp. Instinctively I checked
for blood, saw none, and flashed my eyes back to the lioness. She
hadn't moved.

I risked a glance over my shoulder and saw that in a few steps
I would be at the curio store, which at night was covered by an
enormous sheath made of drop-down, zip-up canvas flaps. There
was a small couch in there where I could quite happily curl up
for a few hours. Later I'd head to my tent, once the lioness had

gone off to do the violent things that lions need to do in darkness. I backed to the store, and as soon as it shielded me from the lioness's view started walking at a normal pace. I quickly covered the walkway to one of the corners, where a large zipper met the timber deck. Bending over, I gripped it and pulled.

It stuck fast. I yanked, and it peeled open with a loud, flatulent sound in the still night air. I stopped the motion a foot from the ground, tried doing it slowly to minimize the noise, but that gave an even louder raspberry so I stopped. I realized the gap I'd created was high enough for me to crawl through. I dropped to my hands and knees, tucked the light under my chin, ready to crawl through. The sideways-slanted beam illuminated the lioness, only feet below me off the deck. She had followed me at ground level and now sat looking up at me with a quizzically cocked head as I struggled to feel more dignified and less like bait. The deck the shop perched on was a man's height from the ground, and while it would be difficult for a lion to make the jump, I had seen extraordinary feats from their species when motivated by fear, food, or even boredom.

This lion didn't seem emaciated, but was lean enough that she would pursue food if it presented itself. She didn't have the demeanor of a lion that had lost its family, nor was she making the mournful deep calls a lonely lion makes. There was only one reason she would be by herself that I could think of. She had cubs somewhere stashed away, and had split from the pride to have them. A lioness with newborns is likely to behave in strange ways and prey on strange food.

But what if she wasn't by herself, and I was just being distracted? What if there were other lions circling, drawing closer, taking advantage of the attention I was paying to their sister? I spun around again, burrowing backwards into the opening I had made in the canvas flaps, and shone my light around the bushes.

We were alone, as best as I could tell. The beam of light seemed weaker, the batteries dying. Not wanting to take any chances, I shifted backwards until my feet collided with something solid. Peering between my legs an ugly and large black face leered back, mouth open, sharp teeth exposed, my foot against its chin.

It was a West African mask, not the sort at all made in Botswana but something tourists would still consider a suitable memento from their trip. I tried pushing it aside, but it wouldn't budge. I visualized the store's layout, and realized that this mask sat outside during the day, along with many other large items, which were then dragged back in at night to prevent them getting spattered with owl poop. The stack behind me, though, meant that I couldn't shelter in the store after all. The couch I had envisioned as a refuge and bed had masks, oversized anklets, and woven baskets all over it.

I focused again on the lioness, the beam weaker, I was sure of it. It couldn't be long before it faded to a sickly yellow light, then blinked out. This would embolden the lioness, which would not be good for me.

Never before had I been hunted and known about it. Tourists often asked what was the closest I'd come to being killed in Africa, and my flippant but truthful answer was crossing the road in Johannesburg. In the bush I wouldn't have known when I had come closest. Any number of times a lion or leopard may have stalked me, a snake may have allowed me to step over it without biting, or a crocodile may have swum close to a bank I was resting on without my having any knowledge of the event. This lioness, though, was definitely sizing me up, slowly overcoming the fear most species have of man, and if I kept giving her opportunities, soon she would take one.

I had to take some initiative. I needed to cross the dip, and get to bed. I wondered who the lioness was. If this was Tippie's sister I would feel more confident, as her pride had an unusual tolerance of humans, but I'd heard that since I'd left Mombo they had been forced from the area and were rarely seen anymore. It could be one of the Matata girls, lions I'd watched for years but never encountered on foot to see how they would react. Night was a bad time to test it.

Striding with a confidence I didn't feel, I moved at the lioness, and walked boldly in her direction, pushing myself against the railing and jabbing the beam at her as if it were a light saber and could somehow repel her. I even added the *zhrroooom!* noises to embolden myself. Whether it was my lunacy or the fear of a seizure from the strobing that did it, she blinked and turned her head away. Her body followed, and she went back into the bushes that she had first appeared from.

I followed her with the beam, still swishing it at her, still making my ludicrous sound effect, hoping that if it did wake a tourist they could only ask the management in the morning whether there was an animal that sounded like Darth Vader and no connection would be made to me. The lioness moved out of the beam's short range, and in the darkness I could just make out a bush twitching as she passed through, in the direction she had originally come from.

The light gave out, the batteries dead.

I still had to cross the open ground.

Clutching the spent flashlight in my untrained fist as a club I kept momentum, not wanting to let fear and doubt overtake me, and strode back along the walkway, back to the dip.

My knees felt like the tendons were giving way, loose and weak as I went. Instinct said I should run the short, dangerous stretch of boards, but I knew that if the lioness was still watching this would trigger her chase instinct, and on the greasy planks I might just as well slip and land on my head, saving her the trouble of knocking me out.

I held my fists in a high boxing stance, and tried to look purposeful and aggressive as I walked down the sloped deck, feeling that indeed it was slimy underfoot. I reached ground level and only had ten yards to cover before the walkway rose, bringing the security of height. Where was the lioness, though? I mostly kept my head turned the way she had gone, but still tried seeing into the gloom to my right as well, not knowing what else might be out there. My neck hairs rose as one of my feet slipped sideways, turning my back to the bushes the lioness had gone into. To not slip again I was forced to a waddle, trying my most to look like a scary duck as I traversed the last few ground-level planks.

"Fool," I berated myself for overlooking the obvious, and took the small step down to the ground, putting the boards between myself and any lion that might charge out, allowing me to walk on soft sand. Any lion could leap the path without difficulty, but the slight barrier allowed some swagger back into my step. I hopped back onto the walkway within a few strides, waddled up the slope to higher path, and tried to see into the darkness once more, but was blind. A herd of elephants could stand there now without my seeing them. I started shaking and only then realized just how frightened I'd been.

I walked the last few paces to the safety of my room, and crawled into bed. But sleep would not come easy that evening, and I listened to the night noises more closely, rather than trying

to block them out so I could rest. The noisy scratchings of a porcupine were clear, and small perturbations in the undergrowth
could possibly have been an aardvark. I'd always felt affection
for these smaller creatures, but now that I knew what it was like
to be hunted, they also had my deepest respect.

THE OKAVANGO DETOX DISASTER

There may be some virtue in abstinence, I pondered, but paralysis took the shine off it. I was considering this in the back of my mind while my frontal lobe tried to figure out what was shaking the low cluster of palms opposite me, and how I would react if it was something that wanted to eat me. Half my body was limp, unresponsive to my urgings for it to wriggle away.

The palms weren't big enough to conceal an elephant, which was some relief, because while they are vegetarians they do on occasion squash people, particularly if said people are silly enough to lie in their way. My relief was tempered somewhat because it could still be a buffalo, hyena, or lion, which certainly wasn't a comforting trio. I used my good arm to drag myself forward, trying to do it stealthily, something difficult when half your body has stopped working. It had been years since I'd had a migraine, and it had escaped my memory just how bad they could be. My whole family was prone to them, and their effect was not unlike a stroke. This one had hit me more than an hour earlier, and I really shouldn't have tried to go for help.

The last time I had a migraine, I'd swallowed some painkillers, slipped into bed, and slid off to sleep. This time instead of acting on the first tingles in my left baby finger, I'd carried on with guide training I'd been sent to a camp named Vumbura to provide. A small school had been set up here in the northern Okavango, and each day I went over the broader points of guiding with the company's new recruits. It had astonished me that I was now, after only six years in the industry, considered qualified enough to teach others these skills (though it had been

213

firmly put to me that I was to make no commentary on the driving of others, as surely it could only be better than mine), and this had spurred an attitude of self-improvement from me. I'd been on a health kick for two weeks.

Gone was the habit of stealing cooking chocolate from the kitchen just for something sweet. No more omelettes for breakfast, instead just fruit and cereal. I was doing push-ups, and sit-ups for the first time since high school, reawakening muscles that pained me each day, as if in revenge for disturbing their hibernation. And in the hardest trial, I'd sworn to go a month without alcohol. This was not just a biological challenge in an attempt to detoxify and lose weight, but a cultural one.

Most guests had a few drinks with their evening meal, some had many. It was easy to join in and find yourself three sheets to the wind for three months straight. Toward the end of the shift it seemed almost necessary to drink the tourists interesting. After a few drinks it was possible to say for the fifth time in an evening, "And you're an accountant too? Fascinating!" and almost mean it.

Two weeks into my detox my skin was clear, my belly less like a hippo's, but the payoff was that the nasty chemicals my system had been storing dumped into my body all at once. This is what had crippled me, and set me off on my ill-considered foray to the main area before dark fell to find, then devour some painkillers. I knew that this would have involved some communicative creativity as my tongue felt like a foreign item, unwilling to do as I bid it. I drooled periodically and it protruded, like a moray eel trying to escape a cave.

The room I was staying in was maybe three hundred yards from the workshop at the back of the camp, and it was only a short distance from that to the first-aid box I craved. So I had set out, sure that even though the left side of my body wasn't responsive I'd know how to walk, based on the memory of having done it more than once before.

Nope. As I pushed out of the low bed I'd been lying on and placed my left foot down, it gave way. I tried again, flopping straight back down and introducing my lip to the rough matting that served as a floor covering.

At this point I should have acknowledged that I was in no fit state to travel, let alone move under my own power, but even at the best of times I ignore common sense and take a running leap from the land of courage to the nation of stupidity. With my head zinging in pain and vision muddled I was even less capable of decision making, so I started slithering, out the door onto the fine dirt of the Okavango.

Using my right arm I'd dig in my fingers and drag, kicking with my right foot. Occasionally my left leg or arm would come out of its strike and let me stagger a step forward, or crawl, and for a while I thought that I was doing quite well.

This triumph dissipated with the fading light, as I knew that dusk would bring out many animals that found nothing unsporting in tackling the handicapped. I kept moving as fast as I could, a debilitated sprint along a narrow track.

Only familiarity with my surroundings allowed me to measure how far I'd come. To my left was high, rank grass that flooded in the winter months but was now drained. To my right was low grass, good grazing for wildebeest, that ran all the way to a dense forest some fifty yards away. Ahead was a plain of mixed grassland that I needed to cross to get to camp, some high turpentine grass already beginning to put out its petroleum smell in the cooling night air, and dry areas of dead grass that grew on sandy patches of ground. I was almost at the plain, but it was here that I needed to pass by the low palm clumps, vegetation that made me wary at the best of times because it was used by many species as a resting place. Now as they shook I cursed my folly, and hoped it was only wind that made them move that way.

"Please be empty," I thought. Then spoke out loud, "pweeze." My lips hung slackly and I sounded silly even to myself.

My entreaties were ignored, and as I drew closer to the clump a frond shook, far too violently for it to have been caused by the mild breeze that was blowing. As if to add emphasis, it shook again.

"Wubber ob!" I said weakly to whatever was wiggling the frond, though what I had intended was a commanding "Bugger off." My pulse raced, and my headache throbbed even worse, something I would have thought impossible. The increased pain made me nauseous.

"Wubber ob!" I said it louder, but the sound was laced with desperation. The palm didn't shake again, just sat limp, menacing. The light went from fading to dim, and I considered that I was closer to my room than to the main area. There was no way that I could get there without being discovered by something like a hyena, and no way I could intimidate it while splayed on the ground unable to swear coherently. There was no guarantee that I would make it back to the room either, but it was closer.

In a break with tradition, I made the sensible decision. I would abandon my plan for narcotic relief and slither back to safety. I turned, grinding my pelvis into the ground like a teenage boy at the beach, and pivoted to start the slow crawl back.

It was tiring work, and I paused to catch my breath, flopping onto my back. The moon hadn't risen, and some stars had appeared, nausea-inducing the way they swung in the sky, so I flopped forward again, almost shoving my nose into the snake that was crossing under my head.

"No way," I said, happy some sounds weren't beyond me, "Webbel by nay!" which was Shlegel's blind snake, but not even an interpreter for the speech-impaired would have picked it. This was a nonvenomous, usually subterrestrial snake that I had only seen twice before, and even in my dazed and pained state it gave me the thrill only the sighting of a rare species can bring. Despite having no functioning eyes and no limbs, the snake elegantly made its way across the grass, as if to mock my progression, before heading into the tall vegetation that was now on my right.

"Bye," I said, and that was actually what I meant.

I tried mimicking the snake's movement to spare my tiring right side, but just flopped from side to side before losing balance and getting a mouthful of soil. My taste buds were sadly all functioning, and there was something in the dirt that I was sure must have been through an animal's digestive process before it made it into my mouth.

I spat, cursed a little "Bubber-ib-pi-wee," before digging in my hand again and pushing off with my heel.

The path was a busy one, and I soon encountered a dung beetle pushing his ball of flavor with his head down and backside up. I'd never bothered to watch one from this level, and now that I saw the degree of effort the little man was putting in, I had renewed admiration for this sewage worker of the savannah. Like a dung ball myself I rolled out of his way until he had passed, then back onto the path.

Despite my weakness, my style of slithering had improved and I was making good ground. Then I was interrupted again. Something was behind me, breathing.

My heart ratcheted against my ribs. This was something big. How hadn't I heard it coming close? A predator would have moved quietly, but it didn't sound like a lion for some reason. Hang on, I reasoned, did I even know what a lion's breathing sounded like? I didn't want to look behind me, didn't want my fear confirmed, didn't like the thought of something leaning in and biting me on the face as I turned.

But I turned anyway, to a beautiful face with a diamond on its nose.

"Hey, zebby," I said, quite thrilled. I'd never been so close to a zebra, and it had come to me! "Wab you booey by yourelb?" (What you doing by yourself?)

It just snorted and pranced away, a high-stepping trot like a creature from a dream.

This was turning into quite a wildlife adventure, and I contemplated how you would market a crawling safari. Probably wouldn't have many takers, I thought, as pain flared behind my forehead, making me gasp, and retch. I spat onto the path, then detoured around the mess. Not far to the door now. I passed some busy harvester termites, already chomping away at grass stems, and watched a firefly blink blurrily as it cruised by with its seductive lamp. I touched the slab that marked the doorstep and felt safe. Paranoia overcame me, and I flipped wildly over to make sure that nothing had stalked me this far.

Nothing.

I'd made it. I pushed through the door which I had mercifully left unlatched and climbed back onto the bed. I lay there for what felt like years, seeing stars again, but knowing they must be imaginary.

Sounds came in and out, hallucinatory, hyenas, far distant

lions, a hippo's snort followed by a splash, voices drifting from the unreachable camp, then footsteps, coming closer.

It was Rob, the camp manager.

"Hey Pete! Want to join us for a beer?"

"Bugger off!" I said, sounding strong. Must be better already, I thought, as Rob trudged back into the night and I drifted off to sleep. I never found out what was in the palms, and never went on a detox again.

CAT AND MOUSE

One false move and I was dead. If I moved too slowly, or too quickly, the elephant would smack me with his trunk, then crush me with his massive forehead, or slide a tusk between the joints in my spine, lift, and toss me like a doll.

My blood fizzed with adrenaline, my nostrils stretched and sucked greedily at the heated air, my hair bristled, my heart rattled at my ribs like a madman in a cage. Every sense was heightened, every instinct attuned to keeping me from being killed. The elephant was determined to destroy me, and all that separated us was three feet, and a leadwood tree. I have never felt so terrified, yet so alive.

The elephant swayed to his left, and, keeping the tree between us, I moved to my right. My tent was about forty yards away. In a flat sprint, it would take me only a few seconds to reach it and the flimsy security it offered. But the ground was not level, and it was covered with low bushes, old spring hare burrows, and rotting branches shed by the trees above. What speed I possessed was of no use, as an elephant would feel no qualms in going right through the obstacles that would impede me, and was faster than all but the most steroid-riddled of humans.

The situation was all my fault. I was guiding full-time again, having found teaching dissatisfying and management beyond my capabilities. It was one of the blissful, rare days where between brunch and afternoon tea I had no airstrip transfers, no strained farewells or awkward introductions with tourists, but instead the opportunity to sleep. I had all but spun the wheels of my Land Rover in the dusty turning circle after brunch, then kicked as much dirt from my heels racing to my room, pouring water on my bed for coolness and flopping onto it in nothing but my shorts, the door loose on its hinges in the hope of a breeze.

But the air would not do any more than slowly flap the sides of my tent, as if the structure itself was breathing, humid exhalations that drew more sweat on my body and whipped none away.

The gauze that represented windows in my tent also moved weakly, and at first I didn't see the elephant. His ears flapped as listlessly as my walls, cooling the blood behind their thin skin and directing it around his massive brain. He wasn't feeding, wasn't moving, which was unusual for an elephant. I watched him awhile, shut my eyes, perspiration running in irritating rivulets from my armpits and brow, pooling and making a salty itch.

I opened my eyes. The elephant was still there, maybe thirty yards from my tent, in the inadequate shade of the knobthorn acacias, leaning against a fallen red bushwillow.

I'd heard for years of a challenge old school safari guides set themselves. These were the sort of guides who looked at us younger ones with our sensitivities, personal hygiene, ideas of equality, and anti-shooting stance as being quite soft. They would creep up on an elephant and pluck one of the wiry hairs from its tail. This would show their stalking skills, ability to confront a great beast, and get away with it. Then they'd probably eat raw meat with their hands, and fill the air with the stink of testosterone.

I'd always expressed disdain for such a blatantly macho task, feeling it not far above a pissing contest. But I'd recently made a very hard decision to leave the bush, and was working through a list of things to see and do before I re-entered a world where people didn't live in tents and were able to do things like watch television for entertainment. With no one to see me, I took the bait, displaying my own weakness for a challenge, and focused on the elephant's tail, my fingers already making clutching motions.

My aim was to move silently, leopard-like, but my door creaked as I slipped past it, and my sandals found every dry leaf. To my ears their popping was as loud as a poacher's rifle. Yet the elephant paid me no mind. He was perhaps deafened by the cicadas whose drone cycled through the air like the sound track to a migraine.

I crept wide around, using what cover there was to break up my form, moving as I had seen cats do, sliding my toes between blades of grass, then slowly easing my weight down. With so little breeze I wasn't that worried about my scent carrying, though my sandals were no source of olfactory delight, and could cause offense as far away as Zimbabwe.

As I moved in, my nerves jangled, and I thought of giving up. I had one piece of open ground to cover, and I couldn't see how to make it across without the elephant seeing me. I knew his eyesight would be weak, as it is with the whole species, but not so weak that he could not perceive a five-foot-nine upright figure closing in. I waited next to a tree, trying to blend in with the bark. The elephant kicked casually with one of his forefeet at the bare ground in front of him, and I knew my chance was about to come. With two more sharp kicks of his block-splitter-shaped foot he had reached cool sand. He gathered the dirt in his trunk and arched it, whipping it back over his head for the sand to pour over his back, cooling him down by some small degree.

I used the cloud of dust as cover, and scrambled low across the open ground, aiming for the fallen log. I angled so I would come in close to his rump, marveling at something I found every time I got this close. Elephants are big. From the safety of a vehicle they may appear large, daunting and powerful, but on foot, up close, they are something else. They tower over everything, radiate majesty, and exude a casual power. They pull the energy from around them, absorb the light, and hold attention like nothing else on Earth.

I hesitated a mere ten feet from his rump, as the elephant turned with astonishing speed, and charged.

"Oh, bugger," I thought. He knew I was there all along. Breaking the golden rule of "Whatever you do, don't run," I sprang from my crouch and took a few running paces. Of the many tidbits of trivia I knew as a guide, the specific density of trees became useful for the first time. A rain tree would not stop the elephant, nor would the feverberry. The leadwood, though, was made of such a heavy timber that its logs did not float, and furniture made from it, while beautiful, was likely to cave in any floor you placed it on. It was exceedingly heavy timber.

Now it was perfect for sheltering me from an angry elephant. I just wished it was a little wider as I stood with it between me and an angry animal. Periodically the elephant would pretend he was going to push the tree on top of me, and his forehead was broad enough to be seen on both sides of it as he leaned in.

"Sorry," I whispered, "I'm sorry." And I was. This was not the meaningless apology of a teenager, but the shame of someone who should have known far better, who professed to loathe cruelty yet was now in a pickle from chasing souvenirs to satisfy his machismo.

No matter my sincerity, the elephant was not having any of it. I kept looking behind me at my tent, calculating the distance, as if through sheer strength of will it might have moved closer. But it never did, and I remained in the trap of my own making.

The volume of adrenaline flooding my muscles had no outlet and set me to shivering. I tried to suppress the tremors, not wanting to show a weakness, but it only led to violent jerking and facial spasms.

Our game of cat and mouse felt like it had lasted for hours, and I was amazed at the elephant's tenacity. Pure instinct kept me alive, my knowledge of elephants useless here as I had never been trained for such a sustained encounter.

He backed off, a full three steps from the tree. He turned side-on, and reached down with his trunk. It probed at the ground, the tactile lips puckering and blowing, before grasping some dried ground cover with remarkable delicacy. The plants furled back to his mouth, and endured two hasty mastications before falling back out. This was mock feeding, and I knew he wasn't interested in his food. He was trying to show that he wasn't interested in *me*, to see how I would react. I had one last surge of adrenaline, looked at my door again, and maybe even leaned toward it a little, then looked back at the elephant. Still pretending he had no interest in me by scuffing at the ground with his foot, his eye gave the game away. It was wide, the heavily veined white of it clearly visible as he focused on my position behind the tree.

Under other circumstances his guileless performance would have been amusing, but I didn't think it was funny. His eye rolled, and I realized that I wasn't able to tell if he was furious, or fearful. It angered me that I didn't know the difference. What was I doing playing these sorts of games, then? I felt a rush of self-loathing that I'd dodged for many years take over me, and exhaustion seep into my bones, curling my knuckles and juicing my veins with fatigue.

The adrenaline was gone, used up by my shakes and shivers,

and now the safety of my tent may as well have been in another nation. Up until now, and in every dangerous encounter I had had with wildlife, a combination of training and instinct had seen me through. Nobody had ever told me what to do when an incident lasted as long as this one had, which by now must have been more than a quarter of an hour. I racked my memory for a way out, straining so hard I feared I'd develop the first case of hemorrhoids on the brain. My instincts were as drained as the hormone that had given me energy. A mad moment came, and I contemplated just stepping toward the elephant, arms held wide, and letting him have me. Why not? Only a few years earlier when I was seventeen I would have done it.

I'd been a morbid youth, moping around and reading way too much Stephen King. I'd never dyed my hair black or had any extremities pierced, as I knew that was too obviously a cry for help, and didn't want that sort of attention. Instead I became introverted until my fascination with what happened after you die became unhealthy, and I decided to find out.

It wasn't just my scientific curiosity that drove me, but a feeling that I had no place in the world. My parents insisted that law or medicine was where my future lay, yet I had no interest in either. My love for animals had no practical application that I knew of, and all I thought of myself was that I was wasting space and resources that could be used by wildlife.

One night I took more pills than any individual should take in a lifetime, but as doctors later told me I have an unusually strong internal structure that absorbed the medication with little long-term effect. "You have the liver of ten men," a doctor told me, something I'm still not sure is a compliment or not.

Within a month of my attempt something clicked, and I made the decision to leave my mediocre school and indifferent home, and was promptly disowned. Despite the joy of escaping unhappy circumstances after I joined the workforce, I soon found myself working like a mule for a life I didn't want. It was merely existing. Not living, just getting by. After two years of this I fled again, this time less dramatically, taking a plane instead of pills. In Africa I realized what a passion for nature I had been restraining, and that the passion had an outlet.

As I stood behind my leadwood shield I had the perfect opportunity to fulfil my aim of only a few years earlier. Yet I couldn't. It would betray the promise I had made to my sister and friends, whom I hadn't expected to be so upset by my attempt. But beyond that promise, at seventeen I hadn't imagined that I could ever be in this sort of position, pegged behind a tree with one of the world's most exciting animals on the other side of it. I was living a life that was far more fulfilling than the one that had been planned for me. Dark days, even weeks, still plagued me, when an enduring silence held incredible appeal, but the spell could be broken. All it took was interacting with a cheetah, or watching a lion cub grow, or being scared witless by an elephant, as I was now.

So I held my ground for what seemed ages, moved when the elephant feinted, and ducked back as he changed direction. Finally he just quit, and with a loud sigh walked off, apparently satisfied he had taught me the lesson I needed to learn.

When he had moved into denser bush, vanishing in the disconcerting way that elephants do, I gripped the rough bark of the tree and gathered my breath.

I walked back to my tent, splashed water on myself, and sat on the bed's edge for a while. In my room were a number of items that I had collected while living in Africa, which I would take with me when I decided where I wanted to live next. I had a monkey's skull, some scales from a pangolin, and a bird book filled with notations. I didn't have any hairs from an elephant's tail, but that didn't seem important at all.

DON'T ASK FOR RED DRUM

After ten years of working in tourism I felt burnt out, left the bush, and took a four-year hiatus in Australia. But I found that an itch for Africa just would not subside, and I had arranged to come back for three months with the one man who would employ me no matter how many vehicles I destroyed or how often I became lost. It had been three years since I had been in Africa, and four since I had last seen Chris. Since I'd left the continent I had struggled to find my place in Australia, my dreams of making enough money to buy a camp of my own far from fruition. Most weeks I barely made rent.

"Good to see you, Chris," I said when he greeted me at Windhoek Airport, and I meant it. I embraced his six-foot-five frame. "I'd like to wear some of your wife's clothes."

"Sure, chap," Chris said, not in the least taken aback. "They lost your luggage, hmm?"

The airline had, and I knew that for the next few days I'd have to be content with the contemptuous stares at my city haircut and soft city hands while wearing a pair of woman's shorts. I hadn't bothered asking to borrow Chris's, as they were large enough for me to stick a pole in and use as a tent.

Yet I was overjoyed to be back. Getting off the plane I had been assaulted by the smells of Africa, which was a welcome attack. As soon as the plane had landed, we had disembarked onto the ground, as is common in Africa, and the aroma of abundant wood cooking fires reached me, as did the scent of the baggage handlers and the Vaseline they rubbed into their skin to keep it shiny.

Chris knew without asking why I was smiling so much, and told me that I was about to enjoy myself even more this time around. "We're sending you to Serra Cafema."

This was a place that is sometimes billed as "The most remote camp in Africa." I had read about it and was thrilled to be going. But Chris hadn't told me yet how I was getting there.

"You fly over the Skeleton Coast, don't you?" I asked, hopefully.

"Hmm," Chris replied, which I took as affirmative.

"Can you see the shipwrecks?" The region was famously littered with the carcasses of unlucky vessels that had strayed too close to the coast.

"Hmm," Chris said again. There was a definite tinge of the negative to this sound, and I knew that there was a loop that I was definitely not in.

"Chris?"

"Hmm?"

"How am I getting to Serra Cafema?"

"You're driving."

"Who with?" The answer to this was critical, as my propensity for getting lost is legendary.

"Hmm?" Chris asked, as if the silence of the desert we were driving through to reach his house had deafened him.

I was deeply jet-lagged after a fifteen-hour flight and felt like the clothes I was wearing had been dipped in soup, yet the dread caused by what Chris was telling me overpowered this discomfort like a slap in the face.

"We'll give you plenty of fuel to take," Chris said, still speaking in a mild tone, as if what he was asking me was reasonable. "And water, in case you get lost." Namibia is bigger than many European countries. In fact it is bigger than many of them glued together, but has fewer than two million people. It is easy not just to get lost, but to stay that way. Maybe I would end up staying in Africa forever, I thought, just because I couldn't find my way out.

I spent a few days in Windhoek, Namibia's capital, catching up with old friends, waiting for my luggage, and slowing myself to the pace of Africa. It was an easy town to be in, well developed and reflecting the country's prosperity. Namibia has a wealth of diamonds in its sand, as well as an abundance of other minerals, and, like its neighbor Botswana, was spending its money with some sense. It was refreshing to be in a place not afflicted with the lunatic governance of so many African nations. Windhoek's civilization was only a gateway to the true, wild country, though, and I needed directions to get where I was being sent.

Chris's office was piled with papers that he seemed to have mainly for decoration, because every time he was asked for a file he gave no indication of knowing where to look for it. "There's a map here somewhere, otherwise there'll be one in the vehicle, but it'll probably be out of date because the rental companies don't put new ones in, in case they get stolen."

"A rental? I'm not taking one of the company's vehicles?"

"Oh man, you wouldn't believe how rough the tracks are to get to Cafema. There are ruts so deep a giraffe can hide in them." I was sure he was exaggerating. I did know, though, that most of Namibia's roads were unpaved, and sometimes went untraversed for years, making them almost impossible to follow as the desert reclaimed them. "Anyway," Chris continued, "the vehicles get so trashed along the way that it's cheaper for us to rent them to take freight and staff out. Don't be surprised if the license plates fall off along the way. Or the running boards on the side. If you feel it happen, pick them up and try to stick them in the back. Listen," he said, pulling out a pen and paper from one of his random piles, "I can't find a map, so I'll draw you one."

I like Chris a lot. He has a great sense of humor, a way with people rarely matched, and is generous to a fault. But one thing he is not, by even the loosest of definitions, is an artist. First he wrote three lines, describing streets named after revolutionary heroes. These would lead me out of Windhoek. From there I would be in an area where the roads became sandy tracks. These tracks had no names. After the three lines of script, he began to draw. The sketch looked like a road-killed snake. Lines spewed intestinally in all directions from a single dark stripe.

"The thicker line is the one you should follow," Chris explained, indicating the bit I had thought was the snake. "Don't follow these tracks," Chris explained, drawing over some of the intestines, immediately making them dark and indistinguishable from the main road. "They lead either into the desert, or into villages where most of the time people are friendly, but in some of them you could get robbed."

"Great," I said. "I can't tell you how much I'm looking forward to this."

Chris didn't look up to check my sarcasm, so intently was he staring at his art. "Hmm," he said. "I might have missed one or two turn-offs here, so just try to stick to the most main-ish sort of track. Eventually you'll find a village called Okahandja. They sell fuel—fill up, because there's no more unless you cross the border and head into Angola." He looked up at me. "Don't do that, by the way. There's still a lot of land mines."

He held his drawing out at arm's length, smiled proudly, and handed it to me. "There," he said. "That's the first leg."

I raised an eyebrow. In Africa, distances are only measured in miles or kilometers if you fly. At ground level only the estimate of how long you'll be on the road matters, as some can barely be driven at a pace faster than a slow walk. Time spent backtracking if one is lost also has to be factored in. This journey would take me at least two days, and would lead me from the center of the country to its most northern reaches, ending at the Kunene River, a place that marked the country's border with Angola.

Chris told me that in Okahandja I would pick up two staff members who might know the rest of the way, but that it was unlikely. He then quickly sketched a drawing of another road-killed animal, this one looking more like an unfortunate hedgehog. Chris told me that from here the road was often swept away by the wind, but I would know that I was on the right track when I saw a sign that said I could be arrested for going any further. "Ignore it, and keep going," Chris said, clearly forgetting that it was he who had been in charge the last time I was arrested. "It's the Skeleton Coast National Park, and there are still some untapped diamond fields in there, so don't stray or you could get in trouble. You just follow this bit," he indicated the hedgehog's rectum, "and you'll reach our camp there. Stay the night, and head for Cafema in the morning."

The third map Chris drew didn't resemble any animal. The sheet was virtually blank, except for a line cutting through it, then a sprout of broccoli, and a can of beans.

"There aren't any real tracks here," Chris explained. "Just follow the plains, in a sort of northwest-ish direction, with a little bit of east every now and then. You'll cut through some low mesas, and drive for about three hours, and then you'll see a tree. Turn left." I was disturbed that the broccoli was meant to represent a tree, but that was not what bothered me most.

"Chris," I said as gently as I could, using the voice I

reserve for people who have just been in a serious accident or anything else potentially brain damaging, "Africa is filled with trees."

Chris just blinked at me for a moment, then said, "Not this part, smart-arse." He then explained that after the tree there was a dry riverbed to cross, then another, then to keep my eyes open for a red drum. When I saw the red drum, I was to take another left. "But," came the addendum, "if you don't find the red drum, then if by some miracle you see someone to ask for directions, whatever you do, don't ask for red drum."

"That's ridiculous, and now I know this entire conversation has been a joke." Men rarely need encouragement not to ask directions. I was sure he was just being a goose.

"Shut up, would you?" Chris said without the irritation most people would have when delivering such a line. "There is a village in the north, and it's called Red Drum. If you ask for directions, they'll send you there."

Right, I thought. Perhaps it was just easier for me to find my way back to the airport and go home. "I'm sure I could communicate that I actually wanted to go to the place where there is a red drum, not to go to the Red Drum that is a place."

"Well, you said that in English, and I barely understood you. How's your Himba?"

"Not a word," I replied, quite honestly.

"Herero?"

"Same."

"Afrikaans?"

"*Ek praat net bietjie*," I said, which means "I only speak a bit." This was less honest. I can pretty much say only that one phrase, which has never been very useful.

"They speak even less. Don't ask for red drum."

Chris explained the last of the route, and said that once I reached the soft sands close to camp I had to let the tires way down, and to be careful not to go too fast when I went over the lips of dunes because the vehicle would be launched over the soft side of the dune, known as a slip face, which was apparently not very good.

I saw the vehicle the next day, already heavily laden with bags of flour, plastic drums of cooking oil, plastic-wrapped trays of tinned food, and drums of diesel fuel that would be useless if I was lost because this car ran on petrol.

"Have fun," said Chris, before waving as casually as if I were just popping down to the store for milk. "If I remember to, I'll check with Skeleton Coast tonight to make sure you got there."

"Great," I said, and set off.

The paved roads quickly ran out, and I remembered why I was so excited to be back in Namibia. I'd spent a month here once before while on leave, and had fallen in love with its contradictions. This was a country of harsh conditions yet alluring beauty. It held places that I wanted to stay in forever yet wouldn't survive a week. It was apparently lifeless, yet animals appeared in the last place you'd expect them—zebras on the mountaintops, baboons in the dunes, even elephants coated red with the dust of the land.

To my great surprise I found the small town of Okahandja quite easily, and two women bustled their way into the car, nodding enthusiastically at me when I asked if they were going to Serra Cafema. I hoped they were the staff members and not just hitchhikers. It struck me that I had no idea what Serra Cafema meant, and maybe I had just offered to buy them some bananas, or give them a blanket for the evening. I really didn't know, but I presumed it wasn't anything offensive as they weren't hitting me with their bags, which were jammed into the overstuffed vehicle so tightly that I was forced to slide my seat forward. With every bump my head hit the roof of the car, and for once on a long journey I wished for one of our game drive vehicles. The women didn't thank me for my consideration, didn't address me at all, and even more strangely didn't speak to each other.

I hit a junction, and glanced at Chris's drawing. It was hard to determine which was the greater mess—his directions or the track in front of me. In what became a regular game of roulette that day I made a choice based on gut, and swung along the track that felt correct.

The landscape changed from scrubby to mountainous, but not the lush montane environment of central Africa. The crags here were dry, with dominant shades of red, ochre, and orange. Sand swirled across the tracks, and crept through the cracked seals in the doors, making my feet skid on the pedals and clogging the fine hairs in my nose. My nostrils began to whistle with each breath, the only music as there was no radio in the rental four-wheel-drive. The two ladies didn't seem to mind.

Occasionally, I would stop the car so we could stretch our legs, and I made a point of turning around and looking closely at the road we had come along. Some years before, in Botswana, I had asked an old member of the San tribe to pass on some of his tracking knowledge, and he had taken me for a walk into the bush. He'd caught me taking particular note of a tree with a conspicuous hole in it as we approached, and chuckled derisively. "You white people," he said, "are so stupid," and laughed harder.

"Yeah, I know," I replied, used to hearing this, "but just out of curiosity, this time, why?"

"You looked at the tree so you could find your way back?"

"Ye-es," I hesitantly admitted, wondering in what way this could be a bad thing. We had been walking while he laughed at me, and now with his small frame he showed surprising strength in pivoting me on the spot with his hands.

"LOOK! BEHIND! YOU!" he shouted each word, as if he was not only telling me, but my whole race. "That's what it will look like when you come back! How else do you find your way home?" From the new angle the tree was entirely different. Each branch held a different angle, and the telltale cavity I'd made note of couldn't be seen. This was a lesson I had carried up to this point, but hoped not to need.

I drove all day, marveling at the scenery, giving a casual wave at the traffic we passed every three hours or so. As the sun set the desert became a kaleidoscope, dunes burning to deep orange as the rocks went from red to brown, finally to black and ominous in the sweep of the headlight beams.

Something glinted ahead, and to my amazement it was the sign telling me to go no further. I went further anyway, excited that I seemed to be on the right track. One of the ladies in the back began to babble, and excitedly gesticulated when we came to a junction.

"Skeleton!" she said, clearly delighted that we had made it to our first night's destination. Maybe word of my geographic incompetence had spread all the way from Botswana, across tribal boundaries, and she had been sitting there the whole drive expecting disaster. Even though she spoke no English, I established that she had worked at this camp before so knew its roads well. I also figured out that the silence while we had been driving was because the two women were from different tribes and had no common language.

We found the camp without difficulty, spent the night, and on the advice of the management that it "was a really long drive" shot out of Skeleton Coast Camp as the sun rose. We left the national park, passing the back of the sign that had warned me not to come in. On the back it didn't offer any message like "Hope you enjoyed your stay, please come back." It seemed it wasn't just the landscape that was inhospitable.

The camp we'd spent the night in was not far from the coast, and had been shrouded in fog as we left. As we drove inland the air cleared, and as always happened to me in Namibia my heart was torn in two. Part of me wanted to stop at every sweep of the road, at every ridge top, at every mountain of granite to take photos, as it was the best view I had ever seen. Another part was just as keen to press on, as I knew that around the next bend was most likely a view just as staggering if not more so. But I left my camera in the back since I was convinced I would get lost and would need all the spare time I could accrue.

The hills flattened out, and soon our vehicle crossed wide-open gravel plains. As the hills withered, life too was sapped. For miles we drove, seeing nothing. Not the nothing tourists complained of sometimes on safari in Botswana, but no grass, no landscape features, no bugs, no birds, no life. It was bland to the point of nausea. Mirages danced in all directions, as erratic as the road's path. Previous drivers had gone around deeply rutted sections, sometimes so widely that their tracks appeared to be junctions. I had no idea where we were, or which fork to take, or if there were forks at all.

I'd seen many shapes appear out of the mirages, long tall people, mountains, bananas, and finally something that stopped shimmering and became real.

"Well, bugger me," I said to myself, "Chris was right." In the middle of this stark and seemingly lifeless place was a tree. It was as incongruous as someone with a nipple growing on their eyelid. I turned left.

The track grew thinner, until I thought it was a mirage I was driving on. The landscape began to change again. We drove through riverbeds, dry as old bone, and clearly only carrying a flow every few years. Yet they held life. Clumps of grass clung tenaciously to the ground, deltas of sand piled against them by the wind. More trees appeared, stunted and windblown, yet birds flew from these as we drove past. Less than three inches of rain a year fell in this part of the world, and I was filled with admiration for every living thing within it.

Almost as much admiration as I had for the people who'd planted the red-painted red drum that shimmered into view, and that we soon passed. It was an eyesore, but offered some comfort that I had, for once, not gotten lost.

Dunes reappeared and the rental vehicle climbed these once I had let the tires down until they were almost flat. I got stuck a few times, and the silence of the ladies in the back sounded like condemnation. Each time I lowered the tires further, added power to the accelerator, and cleared the dune on the next attempt.

The scenery was spectacular, and on many occasions I almost sent us to our deaths by paying too much attention to the view and not enough to how close to a cliff edge we were. So much of my time in Africa had been spent in the Okavango, which is beautiful with its vivid greens and sparkling blue water. This was so different, though. This felt like another planet.

My appreciation of the surrounds was interrupted as one of the ladies burst into Himba, clearly recognizing that we were close to Cafema. I hadn't gotten lost, not once. Was I the same person I once was? It just didn't feel right for me not to have made some grand mess-up, and either wrecked the vehicle or gotten hopelessly lost.

We crested a rise, and below us the stark beauty of the desert was interrupted by a strip of verdant greenery. Here, in the middle of commanding dunes and rugged volcanic hills, was a river. For two days we had driven without seeing water. Here it was in spades. Down here, I had been told, were crocodiles. I allowed myself to stop the car, grabbed my camera, and got out, my emotions threatening to break a dam.

Four years earlier I had left Africa, unsure of whether I still had a place there despite my enduring passion for the continent and its wildlife. My guiding days were over, as ten years in tourism will burn out even the most patient soul, camp management crushed any hope I held for humanity, and being a desk jockey for a safari company was as appealing as hemorrhoids.

Yet I had returned, as almost everyone exposed to Africa eventually does. I had come back to see if I did have a place here, to see if Africa could still surprise me. Even though I knew that this river would be here, to see it made my chest swell with held air. I was at the top, looking down. This is what I came back for, I thought, this is it, and climbed back into the vehicle, shimmying it down a dune, where I promptly got it deeply, deeply stuck in the soft sand at the base. I burst out laughing. "Oh yeah," I thought. "I'm back."

EPILOGUE

Africa has been a teacher to me. Beyond the facts and figures I now know about wildlife, it has made me aware that life can be short and should be lived to the fullest. I learned this from the people I worked with, but also the people I took on safari.

Over the years all sorts of people have sat in my Land Rover. Accountants, lawyers, bankers, photographers, aviators, entrepreneurs, TV stars, mistletoe harvesters (apparently there is more money in that than you would imagine), Germans, Japanese, Americans, English, and every nation in between. Those who appreciated their surrounds and made the fewest irrational demands were rarely as memorable as the nutters who arrive a few times each year astonished that their walls are not concrete and their hair dryer won't work—but from all my guests over the years I learned the heartening fact that people do care about animals. It may not run as deep as the love felt for wildlife by me and my bush colleagues, but that may not be an entirely bad thing.

I no longer live in Africa, but visit regularly, sometimes to lead trips, sometimes just to see friends. People often ask if I plan on returning there to live again. My answer is always ambiguous. All my life I have been afraid of going backwards, and steamed ahead, not wanting to look behind, or dwell on the past.

But there is another thing Africa taught me. It's okay to look behind you. Sometimes it is the best way to get yourself home.

ABOUT THE AUTHOR

Peter Allison is a safari guide who has worked in South Africa, Botswana, and Namibia. It was his love of animals that led him to Africa, and by the late 1990s he was in charge of training guides for the region's largest safari operator.

Safaris he has led have been featured in such magazines as *Vogue* and *Condé Nast Traveler*. He has assisted *National Geographic* photographers and appeared on television shows such as "Jack Hanna's Animal Adventures."

He currently lives in Sydney.

Also by Peter Allison

DON'T RUN, WHATEVER YOU DO
My Adventures as a Safari Guide

Peter Allison works as a top safari guide in the Okavango Delta, an oasis of wetland in the middle of the Kalahari desert, rich with wildlife. As he caters to the whims of his wealthy clients, he often has to overcome the impulse to run as far away from them as he can, as these tourists are sometimes more dangerous than a pride of lions!

Full of outrageous-but-true tales of the people and animals he has encountered – the young woman who rejected the recommended safari-friendly khaki to wear a more "fashionable" hot pink ensemble; the drunk, half-naked missing tourist who happened to be a member of the British royal family; the squirrel that overdosed on malaria pills; the monkeys with an underwear fetish; and last, but by no means least, "Spielberg" the Japanese tourist who wanted a repeat performance of Allison's narrow escape from a pair of charging lionesses so he could videotape it – these hilarious stories reveal Allison's good-natured scorn for himself, as well as others.

Allison's humour is exceeded only by his love and respect for the animals, and his goal is to limit any negative exposure to humans by planning trips that are minimally invasive – unfortunately it doesn't always work out that way, as he and his clients discover to their cost when they find themselves up to their necks in a hippo-infested watering hole! Full of essential wisdom like "Don't run, whatever you do", and "never stand behind a frightened zebra" (they are prone to explosive flatulence when scared!), this is a wonderful and vivid portrait of what the life of a safari guide is really like.

Paperback, 256pp + 16 pp colour photos
ISBN 978-1-85788-501-9, £9.99
www.nicholasbrealey.com

Also by Peter Allison

HOW TO WALK A PUMA
& other things I learned while stumbling around South America

"Plans are usually only good for one thing - laughing at in hindsight. So, armed with rudimentary Spanish, dangerous levels of curiosity and a record of poor judgement, I set off to tackle whatever South America could throw at me."

On his nineteenth birthday, Peter Allison flipped a coin. One side would take him to Africa and the other to South America. He recounted his time spent as a safari guide in Africa to much acclaim in *Don't Run, Whatever You Do* and *Don't Look Behind You*. Sixteen years later he makes his way to Chile, ready to seek out the continent's best, weirdest and wildest adventures - and to chase the elusive jaguar.

From learning to walk a puma (or rather be bitten and dragged along by it) in Bolivia, to finding love in Patagonia and hunting naked with the remote Huaorani people in Ecuador, *How to Walk a Puma* is Peter's fascinating and often hilarious account of misadventures in South America. Ever the gifted storyteller and cultural observer, Allison makes many observations about life in humid climes, the nature of nomadism, and exactly what it is like to be nearly blasted off a mountain by the famous Patagonia wind.

His self-deprecating humour is as delightful as his crazy stunts, and his love for animals – even when they bite – is infectious.

Paperback, 264 pp. + 16 pp black & white photos
ISBN 978-1-85788-566-8, £10.99
www.nicholasbrealey.com